RESOLVE

CAITLIN PRESS INC.

8100 Alderwood Road,

Halfmoon Bay, BC VON 1Y1

www.caitlin-press.com

Edited by Meg Yamamoto

Text design by Shed Simas / Onça Design

Cover design by Vici Johnstone

Printed in Canada

Caitlin Press Inc. acknowledges financial support from the Government of Canada and the Canada Council for the Arts, and the Province of British Columbia through the British Columbia Arts Council and the Book Publishing Tax Credit.

LIBRARY AND ARCHIVES CANADA CATALOGUING IN PUBLICATION

Title: Resolve : The Story of the Chelsea Family and a First Nation Community's Will to
    Heal / Carolyn Parks Mintz with Andy and Phyllis Chelsea.
Other titles: Chelsea story and a First Nation community's will to heal
Names: Parks Mintz, Carolyn, 1944- author. | Chelsea, Phyllis, interviewee. | Chelsea,
    Andy, interviewee.
Description: Includes index.
Identifiers: Canadiana (print) 20189059656 | Canadiana (ebook) 2019008619X |
    ISBN 9781987915884 (softcover) | ISBN 9781773860190 (EPUB)
Subjects: LCSH: Chelsea, Andy. | LCSH: Chelsea, Phyllis. | LCSH: Adult child abuse
    victims—Esk'etemc (First Nation)—Biography. | LCSH: Shuswap Indians—Alcohol
    use—Esk'etemc (First Nation)—History. | LCSH: Shuswap Indians—Esk'etemc
    (First Nation)—Government relations. | LCSH: Esk'etemc (First Nation)—History. |
    LCSH: St. Joseph's Mission (Williams Lake, B.C.)—History. | LCGFT: Biographies.
Classification: LCC E99.S45 P37 2019 | DDC 971.11/75—dc23

RESOLVE

The Story of the Chelsea
Family and a First Nation
Community's Will to Heal

CAROLYN PARKS MINTZ

WITH

ANDY AND PHYLLIS CHELSEA

CAITLIN PRESS

Phyllis and Andy Chelsea, 2017. Photo courtesy the author.

Dedicated to those who suffered, to those who died, and to those who will end indifference and create a new path for us all.

Kukwstsemc!

CONTENTS

ACKNOWLEDGEMENTS

WITH THANKS BEYOND MEASURE TO ALL THOSE WHO CONTRIB-
uted to this compilation and to its stories, to those who gave
of their time and knowledge, and who trusted me to convey
their message.

Gratitude is also extended to the supportive staff at Caitlin
Press, to the many who encouraged me to forge ahead when
fortitude was flagging, and especially to my beloved husband,
James, whose patience and understanding sustained me.

For this was a heart-rending book to write, but one I'm
immensely grateful to have been part of—it has been a learning
experience, a complex journey and, ultimately, a labour of love.

—Carolyn Parks Mintz

FOREWORD

CAROLYN PARKS MINTZ'S UNDERSTANDING OF AND COMPASSION for Indigenous history and culture are one and the same. She fully comprehends, from a journalistic point of view, that there is a story to be told, and in *Resolve*, she has done that—recounting the life experiences of a remarkable couple, Andy and Phyllis Chelsea, and building around those, the history of Canada's First Peoples and their hope for the future. It is important to note that throughout the development of this book, Carolyn has diligently avoided appropriation of Indigenous proprietary data or information.

Carolyn's spirit has been true to her word and is evident *in* her words. Her dedication to telling the truth and to honouring the trust fostered with the Chelsea family extends beyond the book project. The Chelseas' legacy will be carried forward. Their reconciliation efforts will continue through the work of this caring writer.

Supporting Carolyn, an excellent wordsmith and an inspired human being, as well as her new book, is an honour.

I can only think that the Creator has brought us together to be family.

Frank Antoine

2018

Councillor, Bonaparte First Nation

Chief Executive Officer, Moccasin Trails Tours

Director and Board Chairperson, Thompson Okanagan Tourism Association

Member of the Board of Directors, Indigenous Tourism British Columbia

PREFACE

IT IS SAID THERE ARE NO ACCIDENTS IN LIFE, THAT THERE IS A reason for all that happens. In the fall of 2016, after moving from Ontario to British Columbia, an area rich in Indigenous history and communities, I was put by chance in touch with several members of the Chelsea family of the Esk'et First Nation at the Alkali Lake reserve, fifty kilometres south of Williams Lake.

During discussions with language educator Ivy Chelsea about a Secwepemctsín (Shuswap) translation for a writer friend of mine, she mentioned that, for some time, she had been hoping for, looking for, someone to write about her parents' lives. I was soon meeting with Elders Andy (former Chief) and Phyllis Chelsea, getting to know them and they, me, over several hours. During our discussions, this exceptional but down-to-earth couple assigned me a task—to come up with an outline for a book about them and their life journey. We'd then decide if we would embark on the project together.

At a subsequent meeting during which I gave them what I had written, the Chelseas agreed that I should write their life stories, extending me this honour with their blessing. And so this book began.

During the initial stages of my work on the book, I was invited to attend a Yuwipi ceremony conducted by David Blackstock, a First Nations Medicine Man. This significant and moving event, which extended healing to all in attendance, included the opportunity to ask for the Creator's blessing, through David, for the book I was starting. This was unreservedly given to me and was something I sensed during the subsequent ceremony. At the conclusion of this meaningful evening, I was presented with a tobacco tie that had been part of the central altar in this room, which contained many important and sacred items and on which the Medicine Man based the healing process.

Tobacco is one of the four medicinal herbs revered by most First Nations. It is believed to connect humans to the spirit world, to absorb prayers and carry them there, and is used to thank the Creator for gifts.

The tobacco tie sat on my desk, close by as I wrote, a reminder of that special night, the blessing given to this undertaking—and a symbol of the guidance I needed.

INTRODUCTION

"WHERE ARE YOU FROM?"—A COMMON QUESTION BETWEEN non-Indigenous people when meeting for the first time. However, as the Chelseas describe, for Indigenous Peoples the question often translates as "What *land* are you from?" This connection, their necessary link to the soil and terrain of the area where they were born, where they walked, played, lived and loved, is critical to their self-knowledge and personal identity. The resettlement of First Nations to arbitrarily chosen reserves of limited size and location destroyed their roots, ripped out their history. They have yet to recover.

This book project began as the life stories of Phyllis and Andy Chelsea. However, it soon became apparent that it encompassed far more, for their stories of being torn from their families as children, of abuse suffered at residential schools, of the destruction of their culture and of the inherent shaming of their self-worth are a microcosm of a much larger societal system that was doomed to failure from the outset—failure on an unimaginable scale that is ongoing within Canada's borders to this day.

While some take issue with the word *reconciliation* being used to describe negotiations between Indigenous Peoples and the Canadian government, some aspects of early contact were mutually beneficial. Explorers and traders acquired valuable knowledge and essential skills from First Nations, and Indigenous Peoples procured tools and useful items through trading with the newcomers. However, the relationship would soon sour as control and greed became the driving force of the migrants.

The term *reconciliation* implies settlement, understanding, compromise, harmony, agreement and respect—the restoration of something broken—all of which could help heal the relationship between two very different peoples, one that began as nation to nation and devolved to something disparate in all ways.

Whatever was to be written had to include a summary of the what, when, how and why of everything that took place. In order to proceed forward, it would be vital to look back. To correct wrongs, to recognize injustice, it is essential to examine such murky things in daylight, look critically at the harm done.

The Chelseas managed to survive the damage inflicted at residential school only to find themselves within the same constrictive organization—the government-sanctioned, Indian Affairs-managed, council-controlled reserve. Haunted by past cruelties, they struggled emotionally and sought temporary escape through alcohol. Their eventual personal success in life has not changed the fact that much was stolen from them, and much will never be returned.

Considerable information has been revealed in recent years about the untenable conditions under which so many Indigenous

Peoples live, stark evidence of a devastating scheme and its resultant damage. The extensive research and many hours of interviews this book required revealed that Indigenous Peoples in this country were and remain caught within a twisted net of initial deceit, unimaginable harm and ongoing neglect. I was shocked, dismayed and, yes, angry. It is one thing to be made *aware* of something, quite another to *feel* it—still.

TREATIES, LEGISLATION AND THE INDIAN ACT

DEFINITIVE FENCES

It could be said that the arrival on this continent of the early Norse explorers, Bjarni Herjolfsson and Leif Ericsson, followed seeveral centuries later by John Cabot and Jacques Cartier, represented the beginning of the end of the inherent rights, freedom and lifestyle of its Indigenous Peoples.

Initial contact between Europeans and those who had long lived here included diplomacy, treaty relations and trade alliances in areas of mutual interest and gain. However, the expansion of colonies brought with it European conflicts as the French and English vied for control of and economic benefit from this resource-rich land. Military leaders sought and gained the support of Indigenous allies in defending their settlements against invading forces. Indigenous Nations signed agreements and treaties that included trade arrangements, military protection and the right to hunt and fish in their traditional areas.

Significantly, governments and First Nations have interpreted the concept of treaty in two rather dissimilar ways. While the Crown and governing bodies consider treaties to be constitutionally recognized agreements that encompass Indigenous Nations' concurrence to share interests in their ancestral lands, in return for various payments, goods and promises, Indigenous Peoples often understand them as sacred covenants that establish a relationship between nations—between those for whom Canada is their homeland and those for whom it is not. As peoples of oral history, it has been suggested that First Nations understand the binding and sacred elements of treaties within what was said at the time of negotiations, rather than the legalese of the actual documents. And for them, the requisite force of a treaty is affirmed by ceremonies that took place around the deliberations—the Sacred Pipe or symbolic gifts. In addition, they look to their highly respected Elders for interpretation of the intent and spirit of treaties.

It should be noted that any border between the eventual countries of Canada and the United States could only be described as fluid or non-existent up until 1783, for both the Indigenous Peoples of North America and the new arrivals.

The complex and sometimes convoluted treaty process that took place over hundreds of years is presented in Appendix 2 of this book, and includes a long list of treaties and agreements executed and put in place between numerous First Nations and colonial governments in various areas of North America.

The treaty process was eventually driven by the British Crown's desire to acquire more and more Indigenous Land and was complicated further by the greed of land speculators and the expansionist views of the American republic to the south.

With time, treaties and legislation would diminish Indigenous Peoples to a status as wards of the state, with few rights and many rules—described by many as a definitive blow to their self-esteem and pride of place, a knockout punch to their hope for a better future.

THE INDIAN ACT: MORE FENCING

In 1876, over two hundred years of treaty-making would be overshadowed by one all-encompassing doctrine enshrined in the Indian Act, passed by a government that saw itself as the "guardian" of Indigenous Peoples. The act was based on the principle that it was the Crown's responsibility to protect First Nations until they were sufficiently sophisticated—"civilized"—to fully integrate. This legislation gave the federal Department of Indian Affairs control of basically all aspects of the lives of Indigenous Peoples, such as who was "an Indian," land management, band issues, resources and cultural practices.

Amendments to the act over the next seventy years were increasingly obstructive and imposed ever-greater constraints on First Nations. Invasive rulings, such as excluding women from elections, forbidding Potlatches and requiring written permission to leave the reserve, perpetuated paternalistic policy that had evolved as colonial authority overwhelmed Indigenous Rights. Changes to the Indian Act in 1894–95 and 1920 included compulsory off-reserve education for Indigenous children— yet another tactic aimed at assimilation. Seven generations of Indigenous children would be denied their identity within residential schools aimed at extinguishing their traditions, language and spirit.

One of the most egregious policies of the Indian Act involved enfranchisement.[1] As another instrument of assimilation, a legal process first initiated in 1857 was designed to strip Indigenous Peoples of their status, their treaty and statutory privileges and their right to live in their reserve community—in exchange for the right to vote, to own property and to merge with the "free," non-Indigenous populace. The government had hoped that this would be done by choice, with First Nations individuals voluntarily consenting to abandon their Indigenous identity and society. When very few made this choice, the 1876 Indian Act made enfranchisement compulsory for Indigenous People who had served in the Canadian armed forces, who had completed a university education or who had been off-reserve for long periods, even if for employment—and, unfairly, for Indigenous women who had married non-Indigenous men or whose Indigenous husbands had died or abandoned them. All of these people involuntarily lost their Indigenous status.

It wasn't until after the Second World War that the government finally consulted with First Nations for the first time, and it was with regard to changes to the Indian Act. Some political, cultural and religious restrictions were lifted but not the discriminatory loss of status for Indigenous women, whose rights came entirely through their husbands. If they married a non-Indigenous man, they lost everything.

Indigenous Peoples were given the vote in 1960, and significant amendments to the Indian Act in 1951 and 1985 revised segments related to "Indian status" and enfranchisement, thereby eliminating specific prejudicial portions of it that were

---

1   Mccardle, "Enfranchisement"; Crey, "Enfranchisement."

found to be in contravention of Canada's Charter of Rights and Freedoms.

Bill c-31, passed in 1985, sought to address growing national concern over the disparity meted out by the Indian Act. Under c-31, those who had lost status through marriage were reinstated as Status Indians and band members, enfranchisement clauses were removed and bands were given control of their membership.

During 2016 and 2017, following eighteen months of deliberation and consultation, royal assent was granted to a bill adopted by the Canadian Senate and House of Commons, which further eliminated inequitable treatment of Indigenous women versus men with regard to entitlement to Indian registration and also clarified complexities involved with passing on status to progeny.

Introduced in 1999, the First Nations Land Management Act permits eligible First Nations to opt out of thirty-four land-related sections of the Indian Act to develop their own land codes and independently govern their reserve and resources.

THE INDIAN ACT, BY THE NUMBERS:

Length of the act, in English and French (letter size)	87 pages
Number of provisions/regulations	116
Number of related provisions	38
Number of additional regulations made under the act	26

Though an exceedingly negative piece of legislation, the Indian Act has been tolerated as preferable to the surrender of

First Nations' traditional entitlements. Several critical issues appear to be intrinsic to changing the relationship between government and First Peoples in Canada: preservation of unique Indigenous history and customs, recognition of First Nations' inherent rights and title, equitable provision of the essential services available to non-Indigenous citizens, and land settlements and consensus among their 634 bands as to the effective self-governance required to deliver the most benefit and significant improvement to the lives and livelihood of their people.

The language is the culture.
The culture is the land.

—Andy Chelsea[1]

---

1   Andy Chelsea, Esk'et First Nation website, https://www
.esketemc.ca/.

THE ESK'ET FIRST NATION
AND THE PAST

THE PRE-CONTACT INDIGENOUS PEOPLES OF WHAT IS NOW known as North America were resourceful, capable and successful—thriving in harsh environments, using all that nature provided for them and developing sophisticated societal systems.

They believed it was their sacred duty to protect all of nature, to which they were intrinsically connected, and from which came the sustenance they needed to live, to endure. Oral Traditions passed on the stories of their past, their cultural and spiritual values and the essential wisdom and expertise the younger generation would require in the future.

Broad expanses of waterways, land, forests and meadows were their neighbourhoods, freely traversed, intimately known and highly valued. The autonomy to move as the seasons and food supply required infused these peoples with undeniable independence, with a sense of unity with Mother Earth and an alliance with nature that, although truncated by the reserve system, exists to this day.

Pre-colonization life for the Esk'etemc—a First Nation of the Secwepemc—mirrored that of their ancestors until the late

1800s. At that time, the Esk'etemc were rounded up from small settlements along the Fraser River in what is known as Cariboo-Chilcotin (Tsilhqot'in) country today and consigned to reserves, with their children sent to residential school.

In the years prior to this resettlement of the area's First Peoples, the German-born immigrant-explorer Herman Otto Bowe built and managed a stopping house on the original gold trail to Barkerville and Wells, which wound its way through the lush valley southwest of Williams Lake—the land of the Esk'etemc. In 1861, on this route, eventually known as Dog Creek Road, Bowe would establish Alkali Lake Ranch, which grew to 37,000 acres with a 125,000-acre range permit and is now the oldest operating cattle ranch in British Columbia.[1]

The encroachment of the expanding ranch created untold difficulties for the Esk'etemc, who wished to continue occupying their Traditional Territory regardless of the government-ordered restrictions around this.

"Old Mr. Bowe would chase Indians away," reports Phyllis Chelsea, "but we'd keep coming back."[2] Ultimately this led to a confrontation. An Esk'etemc woman, pretending she had a shotgun hidden in her layered skirt, told Bowe she would shoot him if he didn't stop forcing her people off the land they'd inhabited for centuries. "That's why our village of Esk'et is established where it is," she goes on. This story was told to Phyllis by David Johnson, the grandfather of Hereditary Chief and Esk'et First Nation historian Irvine Johnson.

---

1   KnowBC.com, "Alkali Lake Ranch" entry; "The Oldest Cattle Ranch in B.C.," *Canadian Cowboy Country*, 2010.

2   Sage Birchwater, foreword to *Jacob's Prayer*.

Esk'etemc Elder and retired practical nurse Dorothy
Johnson relates stories of Louisa Johnson, who was a Medicine
Woman and midwife for the First Nation years ago:

"Starting when I was about six years old and throughout my
childhood, my mom, Angela George, used to tell me to come
along with a sack when Louisa was picking medicine [herbs],"
Dorothy recalls. "I was to help her carry the medicine that
was picked. Louisa would wear a long skirt, long sleeves and a
kerchief and would only speak Shuswap. We'd go up into the
hills and she'd spread out her blanket and take out tobacco or
cigarettes and smoke, asking the Creator for help to find the
medicines she needed, and she would name the ones she needed
them for. Then we'd head out. My mom would be picking too
in another place.

"Louisa would talk to the plants and again name the people
who needed them. I would think to myself, 'This old lady is
crazy, talking to plants,' but I do this today when I gather medicines. I'd put the herbs in my bag and when we had enough,
we'd return to the place where we started. Louisa would smoke
on her blanket again, thanking the Creator for helping her find
what she needed. She would tell me in Shuswap, 'If you had your
eyes opened, you could see what I see—those from the grave.'

"I sometimes helped Elder Louisa deliver babies even
when I was a child. She'd tell me what to do, put water on
the stove to heat up. She'd stay for a few days after the birth,
washing diapers, helping new mothers because they weren't
supposed to lift."

Irvine Johnson speaks of the story of "Peacemaker," an
Indigenous man who travelled North America in ancient times
and was living with the Esk'etemc during one period, teaching

them spirituality and kindness to each other, and telling them to protect the land and animals.

"The only way we got stories," Irvine says, "was by sitting down and listening. There was no radio or TV. Any travel we did was by horse and wagon so we heard lots of legends and stories from way back during those trips. When we were travelling, my grandfather would repeat the same stories over and over, wanting me to learn them the way he told them. If I tried to make shortcuts to stories, he would tell me, 'No, that wasn't the way I told you.'"

As described further on in this publication, the arrival of alcohol with miners and early settlers in Esk'etemc territory and the 1940s payments of social assistance (welfare), combined with the damage wreaked by residential school upon generations of the Esk'etemc, would take this once proud Nation down a path that brought with it the loss of culture, the loss of history and the loss of themselves. They would eventually heal, but it would take time.

The Nation's website states: "The Creator, Kalkukpe7, has given the Esk'etemc the duty to protect and safeguard our lands, forests, air, water, medicines and the life that they sustain within our Traditional Territory. It is this duty that underlies all interests of the Esk'etemc people. Therefore, the protection of our land is fundamental in order to sustain the next seven generations.

"All of our Rights flow from our relationship to the land. Our lives, our culture and our continued existence as a people are completely tied to the land occupied by our ancestors since time immemorial. Our land is a sacred trust. It is the living body of our spirituality. Our knowledge and our customs are understood and practised through this relationship that protects and ensures our survival. It is our mother, nourishing us in all ways: physically, spiritually, mentally and emotionally.

"There is a reciprocal relationship between the health of the community and the health of the land. The land owns us; if we look after it, it will look after us....

"There are no defined boundaries between First Nations. The Secwepemc communities are united by and through the land 'Secwepemculecw'. These continuing relationships and alliances with other First Nations are based on the Seven Laws from Chief Coyote: spirituality, trust, respect, honesty, generosity, humility and patience."[3]

In 2017, the Esk'etemc voted to withdraw from treaty negotiations with the British Columbia government that had been ongoing for over twenty years and issued a Declaration of Title and Rights over the Traditional Territory of Esk'etemculucw. The declaration refuted governmental authority over their communal and land entitlements and stipulated that any development or resource extraction within the Esk'etemc traditional homeland would require their "free, prior and informed consent" and must respect their laws—with the intent of building "positive, healthy and healing relationships."[4]

---

3   Esk'et First Nation website, https://www.esketemc.ca/beliefs-and
     -philosophy/.

4   "Esk'etemc Declaration of Title and Rights," Esk'et First
     Nation website.

I wasn't going to become a white person because someone wanted me to become one.

—Andy Chelsea

It's always been the story of the people of Alkali Lake. I just happened to be part of it, happened to sober up before the others.

—Phyllis Chelsea

THE CHELSEAS' STORY— ANDY AND PHYLLIS

BEGINNINGS

ON MAY 21, 1942, IN THE RIVERSIDE CABIN OF HIS GRAND-mother, Christine Sam Charlie, a baby boy was born to Patrick (Pat) Chelsea and Anastasia Charlie, the fifth of their nine-teen children. The boy was named Andrew but would always be called Andy. However, his First Nations name, Qluwenk, would prove to be especially prescient, would in some ways predict what was to come—for *qluwenk* means "hill or knoll where no grass grows, where the wind always blows." And Andy Qluwenk Chelsea would, with a stalwart woman, one day bring the winds of change to an entire community.

Pat Chelsea was a member of the Esk'et First Nation but worked at the sprawling Gang Ranch adjacent to the mag-nificent Fraser River canyon in Cariboo country. Cowboying was definitely Pat's calling—he was good at it and enjoyed the ranch's open-spaces lifestyle. Also, there he met Anastasia, who was from the area.

The ranch's unique name originated from the fact that it was one of the first outfits to use gang plows to turn the sod and employed large gangs of men to maintain ranch operations.

The cowboys began calling the spread "the Gang" and the name stuck.

When asked what family life was like on the ranch, Andy replies, "It was all fun. Nothing but fun. And I learned everything from my parents, starting with surviving. We learned how to use guns, how to hunt, how to butcher. We needed horses, and so by the time we were age twelve, we knew how to break horses, the wild horses from the area."

But eventually his dad wanted to relocate. The family moved to the Alkali Lake reserve, and Pat was hired on at the nearby Alkali Lake Ranch. For young Andy, the move proved to be less than positive; in fact, he says, it is his saddest childhood memory. "Things really changed," he recalls. "On Gang Ranch, we could saddle up and go anywhere. The reserve had rules and regulations. We were restricted."

One of Andy's happiest memories is the time from age six to eight when he lived with his maternal grandmother, Granny Christine. Although his siblings and parents were close by, and there were regular visits with them, an important part of Indigenous customs involves broadening and nurturing familial connections. Splitting away from their family of origin and residing with grandparents or aunts and uncles presents an opportunity for children to discover, in a new way, the values and beliefs of their people, to hear the stories, to absorb history, to learn more about themselves—and to do all this with someone other than their parents.

"Granny taught me so much about our culture and history, and about nature, how to look after animals, even wild animals, to respect them, not just slaughter them," Andy says, "so much that I needed to know."

And Granny Christine was part of one of the most meaningful First Nations practices significant to the development of a young person—the fast. She took young Andy up into the surrounding mountains, where they spent four days in isolation with neither food nor water. "I learned how to listen and watch what was all around me," says Andy. "Granny was simply there with me. She sat quietly, humming a song and perhaps sewing gloves, not saying too much. I sat by her and observed everything—insects, plants, trees, leaves. I heard the whistling that came through the grasses in a new way. It was never the same from day to day. When I awoke in the morning, emerging from warm hides and blankets, there were always new things to explore. Life was new every day. I began to understand why observing and listening was important to protecting myself. And it was also the time I came to know my spirit animal, the deer."

At one point during that time together—fasting, learning, listening—Granny pointed to their village below and told Andy that one day he would be Chief of his people. But more importantly, the fast and its test were critical preparation for what was about to happen to the child Andy, to Qluwenk, for it had taught him to be strong.

* * *

Born February 2, 1943, to Lily (née Johnson) and Pierro Squinahan, Phyllis Squinahan Chelsea was called Little Sister (Tsetsecen) within her family—and though diminutive to this day, Little Sister would prove to be a pillar of strength for those around her.

A marriage arranged by Lily's family had brought her and Pierro together. Phyllis reports that when it was time for her mother to marry, she was brought by wagon to St. Joseph's Mission. She didn't know the man but knew she was to be married to him by the priest that day. "I asked Mom, 'Holy smokes, what did you do when you were married to someone you didn't know?'" recalls Phyllis. "'Well,' she said, 'I had to live with him then, so I got in the wagon and we went up the meadow.'" And that's where Lily would live for the rest of her life, bearing her four children there: Lorraine, Gordie, Phyllis and baby Morris, who died at a few months of age.

The first six years of Phyllis's childhood can only be described as ideal—a perfect time when a child could thrive, living "up meadow" year-round within her father's family land, east of the Fraser River on what has become part of the Alkali Lake reserve.

"It was a fun time," recalls Phyllis. "There was no alcohol, and we were in the meadows most of the year, living in a log house, going to the reserve about once a month for church, also at Christmas and Easter—my mom and my granny were church leaders—and possibly to Williams Lake once a year. We travelled by horse and wagon; my parents always had a wagon. Dad took care of our food supply through fishing, hunting and the cattle we had then. And we stayed up the meadow, our home place, for the winter season. We didn't like reserve life."

Phyllis's dad, who was the youngest of thirteen children, had a strong work ethic, was always working. His parents had died when he was rather young, and he was raised for a number of years by Alkali Lake's Chief Samson. "What I knew of that Chief," recalls Phyllis, "is that he was chosen by the Catholic church to oversee the goings-on of the church within the community. I understood that he took direction from the priest and was stern with those who broke the rules."

Pierro would also live with another Elder. "My dad grew up to be independent and strong because it was a hard life," Phyllis says. "He had a strict upbringing, and in no way was he spoiled. Dad told me he appreciated it all, though, and had no ill feelings about how he was raised."

And perhaps it was Chief Samson and the Elder who were able to keep Pierro on the reserve, away from residential school and all the negativity that came with that dark period of First Nations children's lives.

"My dad was a good father," says Phyllis. "And he was a famous horseback mountain racer known everywhere. However, during the forties and fifties, as did so many others, he got involved with alcohol and that led to our loss of him. Dad rarely travelled to Williams Lake, but one day in October of 1971 he went into town—and just disappeared. Sadly, he didn't return home and we never saw him again. The police didn't really care about missing First Nations people, especially back then—we never learned what happened to Dad and he was never found. Many from the rez searched for him too. He was gone."

Phyllis was especially close to the maternal uncle who, along with his wife, had raised her mother. Charlie Spahan was definitely Phyllis's grandfather figure, her favourite grandpa. He impressed on her the importance of family, that regardless of circumstance, family was family. This was significant because Phyllis's mom had been born to a single mother, Phyllis's grandmother, Inez, who was just seventeen when Lily arrived. And such a birth was disparaged under Catholicism and in First

Nations societies. Mother and child were considered problematic within a community and society that was heavily influenced by the church. The hypocrisy of this was to become clearly evident to Phyllis in the years to come.

Grandpa Charlie also taught Phyllis about working as a team, whether it was building fences, fishing or hunting, whatever needed to be done at a given time of year. "We often went with Grandpa to do many of those things," says Phyllis. "Work didn't seem like work when it was done together."

In her early years, Phyllis also learned to honour herself, to treat herself—her hair, her body or any of the ways she cared for herself—with respect. She was also taught to respect the land and its animals. "There were wild horses in the meadows, and if I could round up a horse, gentle it, train it, then it belonged to me. It could be mine if I put in the work to make it so. Such things were what my family promoted and stood for, and what we pass on to our grandkids today," she says.

Life up meadow created Phyllis's happiest childhood memories, such as dancing with her dad on Friday nights to music from a Calgary radio station beamed into a large radio powered by a big battery, as well as the freedom of the meadows and the daily opportunity to get in touch with nature, learn about plants, animals, water and earth—all that was and still is so important to First Nations peoples. The meadows were the ultimate playground for a child.

The onset of home brewing and the availability of alcohol by the mid-1940s brought unhappy changes to family life, even up meadow. "There was just one sad incident that I remember," says Phyllis, "when I was about five. Dad and Mom had been drinking and got into a nasty fight. Dad was dragging Mom by her hair and I was following them, kicking at him. My yelling alerted relatives who were our next-door neighbours, and they came and stopped the argument and rescued my mom. I was glad that was the only time such a thing happened."

But by about age seven, Phyllis's mostly happy world would take a sudden downturn. She would experience two tragic events that would forever mark her. Beloved Grandpa Charlie died, at a relatively young age. "It was the hardest thing ever for me," she recalls. "I never really knew how he died; I never asked. My mom would only say, 'When your grandpa died …' and couldn't go any further than that. It was very hard for her too."

The next dark event would involve an open livestock truck, a cold day, many tears and young Phyllis's shock at what was happening to her.

RESIDENTIAL SCHOOL

DESCENDS

CANADA'S RESIDENTIAL SCHOOLS HAVE BEEN THE TOPIC OF many books and dissertations. What has been disclosed is disturbing, saddening, nearly unbelievable.

The "schools" established by the government to assimilate Indigenous children into European-Canadian culture and religion were far from what First Nations leaders had envisioned and expected.[1] The intent of treaties and the interests of First Nations were totally lost in the execution of the mandate. There was no skills-based education. Instead, Indigenous children became the objects of a hard-line, Christian-based integration campaign, supported by the state.

The collaboration between missionaries and government was built on economic expediency; established mission school buildings could be used in many areas, with the government ostensibly providing maintenance and the churches supplying teachers and lessons.

---

1   Miller and Marshall, "Residential Schools in Canada."

Government policy that linked funding to enrolment resulted in sick children being registered to increase numbers and, therefore, the subsequent introduction and spread of disease. Overcrowding and illness became the norm.

Residential schools were grossly underfunded, receiving only a fraction of what was provided for non-Indigenous education. Hence, those hired to teach and supervise Indigenous children were unqualified or at best poorly trained. Curricula were based on materials from a culture alien to the students. As well, maintenance and repairs at the cheaply built schools were severely lacking. Buildings fell into disrepair, were cold and damp and bordered on unlivable.

Governments continually attempted to transfer the monetary burden of running eighty nationwide residential schools onto the churches and the students. Forced labour by students would become (and was) necessary to the functionality of the arrangement and the facility that held them captive.

Very few residential school students can recall positive experiences at what became a form of incarceration, but there were some. It is reported that in rare instances, kind and involved teachers or supervisors tried to provide meaningful education and to make life more bearable for the youngsters, but they were often thwarted by understaffing and heavy workloads.

Andy Chelsea's sister, Marlene, has vivid memories of residential school: "My granny said to me, 'When you go there, learn what you need to learn and leave the rest. Only take the good. Don't bring the bad home with you.' I wondered what she meant then—I was just six years of age—but now I know and understand. And on the day I was leaving for school, Andy told me, 'Never let them see you cry, or they'll hurt you.' I cried alone there, and still do today. It's inbred in me now. Imagine a young child getting that kind of advice, but it helped me find courage.

"Our large family of children had two generations in it. The older ones were grown up by the time the younger ones were born. The older kids like me know what we went through at residential school, but the younger ones who went to school in town by bus know nothing about St. Joseph's Mission. The abuse started the day we arrived. We were away from family for ten months every year. Think about how hard it was for our parents when a priest would come and pick us up, walk away with us, and they could do nothing. We blamed our parents for letting us go when we were young because we didn't know why till later. They hadn't told us about the threat of prison.

"As an adult, I felt I wasn't a good mom. But I didn't have a mom for much of my childhood. How could I know how to parent? I wasn't parented. I was traumatized.

"A bit of what happened at residential school was okay. We had one teacher that I liked; he was English. I still talk about him sometimes. He was an artist and made school fun. And there was a sister who taught grade four who was one of the best nuns I remember. They were the only two who were okay."

Both Andy and Phyllis also would eventually attend St. Joseph's Mission School, one of the most notorious institutions in the system. Located a few kilometres from the town of Williams Lake and dating from 1891, it was the scene of countless incidents of abuse inflicted on the area's First Nations children for decades. In 1991, its dormitory-administration complex, once a three-storey facility for nearly two hundred children, was a faded, whitewashed concrete block building, vacant and vandalized. The five-hectare site had also consisted of an eight-classroom school, a gymnasium, an outdoor swimming pool and seven staff houses.

It was the setting of many stories of humiliation: children forced to wear a sign that read "bed wetter," boys made to wear dresses, girls made to wear diapers, runaways who were caught and whose heads were shaved, as well as reports of beatings with leather straps on small hands and bare bottoms, delivered by priests and nuns, who didn't stop until the child cried or pretended to cry.

The testimonies of hundreds of residential school Survivors recounted abuse that would result in criminal charges if inflicted on an animal, let alone a defenceless child. The litany of assaults includes needles pushed through tongues, faces being rubbed in human excrement, force-feeding of rotten or maggot-infested food, being stripped naked in front of others, immersion in ice water, confinement in closets, hair being ripped from heads, electric shocks and being forced in winter to sleep outside or walk barefoot.[2]

Worst of all, the pervasive and ongoing sexual abuse remained the dirty underbelly of St. Joseph's. It is no wonder that so many students attempted to run away from such darkness, fear and hurt, trying to go home, often caught and punished, or found collapsed and taken by cold and hunger. Eventually, in the 1990s, a few priests would be convicted and serve short sentences, something Andy and Phyllis believed fall far short of what was warranted.

---

2   Spear, "Indian Residential Schools."

The trauma of residential school affected not only the victims, but their families and future generations as well. Andy and Phyllis experienced this intergenerational damage within their own families and witnessed it throughout their community.

Intergenerational transmission of shock and suffering is described in detail in a 2015 paper on the complicated issue of historic trauma by William Aguiar and Regine Halseth, funded by the National Collaborating Centre for Aboriginal Health and the Public Health Agency of Canada, and entitled *Aboriginal Peoples and Historic Trauma: The Processes of Intergenerational Transmission*. The publication discusses a new form of post-traumatic stress disorder (PTSD) known as complex PTSD, which has emerged to address the more convoluted effects of chronic exposure to trauma.

According to the authors' research, the behavioural patterns and characteristics of trauma victims that can contribute to intergenerational diffusion are varied and multi-faceted. These may consist of traumatic bonding, cycles of re-enactment, apprehension, abuse of power, hypervigilance, depression, family violence and toxic emotions. Interacting with physiological and psychological processes, these can perpetuate transference of trauma within families and communities.

* * *

The residential school system would ultimately come to an end, though not soon enough for the thousands harmed by it.

When Canadian Senator Murray Sinclair, the first Indigenous judge appointed in Manitoba and the second in Canada, and former chief commissioner of the Truth and Reconciliation Commission of Canada, was asked why Indigenous Peoples can't "just get over" their residential school experience, his answer is: "Why can't you always remember this? ... Why don't you tell the United States to get over 9/11? Why don't you tell this country to get over all of the veterans who died in the Second World War, instead of honouring them once a year? ... It's because it's important for us to remember. We learn from it."

Andy's father was able to avoid residential school because, from a young age, he was working in the hills on the far-reaching Gang Ranch acreage—the authorities simply couldn't find him. However, his mother, Anastasia, was not so fortunate. Her childhood was spent in what has proven to be one of the most misguided, damaging and negative institutional environments ever conceived. She tried to prepare Andy for what was to come but found it very difficult to describe to her young son the extremely hurtful environment he was about to enter. At the same time, she had been convinced by authorities that the school's "education" was necessary—not to mention the ever-present threat of incarceration if parents did not release their children to the authorities.

Besides being forced to see their young children taken away, most of them crying, parents suffered economic hardship. Family allowance payments were cut off once kids were moved to residential schools. Even though he had worked all his life, Andy's father had to sell his livestock to maintain the household—while at the same time, the mission school was being paid for each child kept there.

Andy recalls that the first real information he heard about residential school came from his brother, when he returned from the school during the summer. "After the first school year, he wanted to run away in September so he couldn't be found and be returned there again," he says. "My brother was really angry about it most of the time, told me he wasn't allowed to speak our language, the food wasn't good. I soon realized that school had to be a bad place."

Andy says he can't remember much about when he was taken away or how he got to the residential school. "I've blocked it all. It was just too traumatic. I do recall that stock trucks were our 'buses,' going from rez to rez picking up kids. It was dusty, sometimes raining and cold, but an open truck transported us."

Local community priests were complicit in locating children for Department of Indian Affairs officials and the Royal Canadian Mounted Police (RCMP), for they knew to which families kids belonged and where they lived. In due course, they led the collectors to the children.

Arrival at the Mission (as students called it) meant more shock for eight-year-old Andy. "I had long hair in braids and was wearing a buckskin vest made for me by my granny," he recalls. "The English being spoken was just noise to me, confusing noise. And then I was grabbed by the neck and put on a high chair. They cut off all my long hair. The vest was ripped off me; pebbles flew from it. My hair and the vest were thrown into a furnace. They seemed to burn forever. I could smell the burning. And I heard my granny's voice saying 'Be strong!'"

And during that alarming introduction to life at residential school, Andy became Number Twenty-One—no longer an energetic, inquisitive lad loved by his family. No name, no identity, no self, as far as those in authority there knew or cared. Thus began nearly eight years of "the war," as Andy calls it, along with his growing anger at the authoritarian, unfair and never-ending rule under which he had to live for ten months of each year until he left that conflict zone at age sixteen.

"Once we walked through those school doors, we became nothing more than a number," he says. "Twenty-one was on my uniform, on my bed in the dormitory, on everything I had to touch. And the daily routine was the same every day. Get up, line up to use the bathroom and wash. There wasn't a lot of time, so we had to be quick, and hope to be near the front of the line because the hot water would run out after ten to twelve boys. Cold or not, you still had to use it.

"Then it was line up again, say a prayer, go to breakfast and pray again, before and after the meal. Dishes had to be gathered up and taken to the kitchen and separated for the dishwashers. After that, we had about fifteen to twenty minutes to brush our teeth, get ready for school. Line up, pray and get to the classroom. Class time was from 9:00 a.m. to 3:00 p.m., with lunchtime of about an hour."

The classroom was just a blur to Andy—he knew nothing of the English language. "I didn't pay attention," he says, "couldn't pay attention. I remember playing with a pencil."

That was when the teacher grabbed him and hauled him to the front of the class. "I spoke Shuswap to her. Then she yelled at me and hit me with a large strap. I let the teacher hit my hands, held them out to her and watched her face. I did not cry. But she did. That's when I laughed." The subsequent beating by an Oblate brother who whipped him all over did, however, force little Andy to cry.

"I stared at that classroom teacher for three days straight, the whole time I was in her room. It spooked her. And I was put in the corner for three days.

"It became my goal to be strapped every day, and I was successful at that. I could control nothing at that school, but that was one thing I could make them do. And sometimes the other boys and I would see who could go the longest without getting strapped."

And then there was the hard work. The students were con-scripted labourers made to split wood, shovel coal, haul wood indoors, care for livestock, harvest potatoes and load produce into cellars. "The worst part," Andy says, "was that the nuns and brothers simply stood around, doing nothing but yell at us, telling us to do it all faster. A lot of anger stemmed from that. We were treated like slaves."

"Slaves" who were fed poorly. None of the fruits, vege-tables and meat made it to the tables of students. "The food was terrible," says Andy. "I can't discuss it. But we had to eat what little there was or go hungry."

He tells of how boys would slaughter and devour anything they could find: wildlife or even livestock if they got the chance. They were starving and didn't care if they got caught.

A friend at school began teaching Andy English orally, and his older brother, Fred, helped with classwork. "I learned very little except to speak English, and I was relying on Fred's help with assignments. I guess I was cheating but I didn't care. I was interested in nature. My cultural knowledge meant more to me than math or language. Two slightly bright spots at residential school were hockey and rodeoing when I got away from that school, but basically I was taught nothing useful there. The only place where I learned was at home."

Fred became the defender of his younger brother. If a fight broke out, he was at Andy's side. And this role of brotherly protector resulted in a dreadful beating for both boys, when the unjust rage of a priest bombarded them.

"I became sick during my first school year," remembers Andy, "and was very cold in bed. My brother, who was in a nearby bed, came and kept me warm by climbing in with me and bringing his blanket.

"In the morning, I was wakened by someone grabbing the blankets from the bed—and me. The priest strapped the hell out of me. Then he turned to Fred and beat my brother until his bowels gave way. All this in front of the other boys. And they made Fred and I fight each other, claiming there was something sexual about being in bed together. Native children often sleep together at home to keep warm. As Fred said, 'If they think we were doing something bad, it's because *they* are doing something bad themselves!'—they were! And my brother and I were made to sleep in separate dormitories from each other."

The trauma of being beaten was heightened by seeing other students regularly beaten. Andy recalls a story about a boy who could shoot a hockey puck like no one else on the team. The other boys' name for Henry Christopher (Chris) Johnson was "Superman."

"One really cold winter day, we were told to go outside by the priest," says Andy, "and we decided to go sliding on a hill. Before re-entering the school, we had to be sure to brush the snow off our clothes. Chris had snow all over, from the knees down, that he hadn't cleaned off.

"When the supervising Brother saw this, he grabbed Chris and threw him across the hallway, where he hit his head on a large steel post. Then he was tossed against a cement wall. After that, he walked in an odd way, was unsteady, couldn't skate. Chris was never taken to hospital. He staggered out of that school years later, still injured, but always worked at Alkali Lake Ranch. Superman was permanently damaged by that supervisor and ended up in a wheelchair."

As is well known and reported, the mistreatment at residential school was not only emotional and physical. It also included sexual exploitation and molestation, infinitely damaging and unconscionably hurtful.

The school's priests and nuns began sexually abusing Andy during his second year, when he was nine years old, and continued until he was a young adolescent and could fight back. Several times a month, day or night, he would be forced to endure this corrupt mistreatment.

"We were afraid every day, as soon as we woke up," he says. "Couldn't concentrate when we were doing chores. If you were alone, you could be victimized. It especially happened when we were showering. And boys were often taken from their bed at night. Besides the abuse, the teasing afterward was nasty— all the other kids knew what took place. It meant you had to defend yourself, fight to keep your self-respect.

"When I was an intermediate boy, a priest abused fifty-seven of us in one afternoon, all of it in the shower. He said he was 'cleaning' us. No, he was sexually abusing all of us! We wanted to kill him. And it happened a second time. He was charged in due course and given a two-year sentence. We were sentenced to a lifetime of remembering.

"One day a friend, who would be my future brother-in-law, and I were running on the stairs at school and there was what looked like a black mound on the landing—a priest and a nun were under it."

Once boys reached adolescence, some of them began sexually abusing younger students—and their priestly supervisors moved on to younger boys. Fortunately, Andy was not subjected to this harm from his peers, but psychologically and emotionally, he had shut down. "When I got older, I climbed into a hole. Didn't talk much. I was just trying to stay alive, to hang on to get out of there," he says.

"A supervisor changed things for us older boys one day, changed our attitude," Andy adds with a wry smile. "He grabbed a boy by the ear and yanked it hard. Big mistake! We were on our feet. We'd had enough! Boys were flying around the dining room and kitchen and going after the supervisor. We fought back. We were ready to riot."

After that incident, an Indian agent (a government representative responsible for enforcing the Indian Act on First Nations reserves) came to the mission and instructed that if kids couldn't be controlled, they should be sent home. Six were sent home. The Department of Indian Affairs hired new help who were to provide stricter supervision, but their attitude was somewhat different, according to Andy. They realized the older boys would fight back, so they were more careful. And they made sure they were never on their own when they doled out discipline.

"As a teenager, I asked my dad if the Chief and council would believe what was happening at the mission school," he recalls. "My uncle was on council. But Dad hadn't gone to residential school. And he told me there was nothing that could be done about it. Band council would do nothing! My drinking started around that time. It was 1958."

Andy Chelsea was sixteen years of age.

* * *

"I don't remember hearing about residential school before a big cattle truck arrived one day," recalls Phyllis. "I was about seven years of age, was put in the back of the truck and couldn't believe that my dad was just going to leave me there!

"Hanging on to the rails and really crying as we left the reserve—everyone was crying—is what I remember most. I just had on a dress and a sweater and it was cold. What was happening to me? What was it all about?"

With an edge to her voice, she says, "The government and the churches were responsible for residential schools, but one group has been left out of the scenario around the removal of children, and that's the RCMP. The priests knew where the children lived because they carried out their baptisms, and they sent the police to their homes. Yes, the RCMP were following the law, but the way it was done, it felt like punishment for who we were. And they've never apologized for their part in wrenching us from our families."

En route to the mission school, at least an hour from the reserve, an interesting incident took place that day. The cattle truck full of children came upon another truck parked across the centre of the road. Its driver, a white man, demanded that the driver get a bus to take the children to the school and ordered him to get the kids off the truck. "We were parked there for a long time until the bus came," Phyllis recalls, "but we were glad to be driven to town in something warmer."

Phyllis says she was allowed to take two sets of clothes and her own shoes and jacket with her to the mission school. "But when we got there, they took it all away, put us in an old uniform and never gave us back the clothes we'd brought with us. I didn't understand why I couldn't wear my own shoes and remember being given shoes with holes in the bottoms. Made me feel so ashamed and hurt. One of the shoes had a big hole in the sole, and I'd try to hide it with the other shoe when we were kneeling for Mass.

"The other tough thing was that eventually we often had to work outside in the yard, and there would be mud and animal droppings all around. I'd try to find cardboard for inside my shoes, but that wasn't easy. Having the muck leak through the old shoes and onto my feet was so humiliating. For years and years, I couldn't talk about these things without crying."

To this day, a new pair of shoes, even if inexpensive, makes Phyllis feel special—she walks with added confidence in them and continues to try to obliterate the terrible memories of having to wear wretched shoes in a wretched place.

"When we first arrived at the mission school, we were herded in a group," she recalls. "Like Andy, each of us was given a number and had to change into the uniform clothes with our number on them. We had to take very good care of those rough clothes, which we were only allowed to change once a week. And I live with the number forty-three every day of my life."

As with all First Nations kids at that time, the language spoken at residential school was upsetting and confusing to

Phyllis. "The only English words I knew," she says, "were *yes* and *no*, and that didn't take me too far." And it wasn't just one language they were subjected to; there were two—English and French. "So while there were those in charge who could speak something other than English, we were forbidden to speak our language. I just couldn't understand that."

It would be a month or more before Phyllis would begin to comprehend English through watching what others did when commanded to do something and with the help of her older sister, who would have to whisper a translation from English to Secwepemctsín (Shuswap). Punishment for speaking their own language could be a strapping, standing in the corner, not being given lunch, losing free time or being forced to kneel on a cement floor for an hour.

And then there was the ongoing Catholic indoctrination—all carried out in Latin. The children simply learned to repeat it, not knowing what it meant or what they were praying about in the first place. Everything was simply done by rote.

In due course after their arrival, the anxious children would be shown to a dormitory—a large, barren room filled with many cots. The warm atmosphere of their family home gone. Their parents gone. Life, as they'd known it, gone, except for two months in the summer and two weeks during Christmas. Phyllis would ultimately endure ten years of this hardship.

The daily routine was just that, she adds, and highly regimented. Any deviation from the usual was unheard of and definitely not allowed. All the youngsters soon became labourers to keep the school operating, their weekdays filled with chores and a few hours spent in the classroom, where they were often taught by unqualified individuals, trained only in religion, who were proselytizing rather than educating.

"We had the same schedule as Andy and the boys: wake up and get up quickly with the bell," recalls Phyllis. "Then it was morning prayers, getting dressed, marching to the dining room, lining up by our place, prayers, a tasteless breakfast, more praying, and then we were assigned washing and drying dishes or setting the table again.

"The meals were awful! Not at all what we were used to eating at home: meat, fish and vegetables. And the school food wasn't cooked properly. Eat it or go hungry was our only option."

After their bland, minimal breakfast, girls did housework and cleaning and attended sewing class, where they often mended school uniforms, before lunch. Class time was from 1:30 to 3:00 p.m. "It was all about lining up, praying, standing still and working most of the time," reports Phyllis. "There was little time for play and no time for freedom."

The weekends with no classes were filled with religious ritual and instruction, along with extra chores that constituted hard work for children and were always under strict, demanding supervision.

"And we were hungry most of the time," reports Phyllis. "The boys sometimes hunted ducks when they were older—once, they even killed a pig and ate it—but the girls had no options, no way to get additional food. We learned how to starve there. If a girl was hungry enough—and brave enough—to steal an apple or piece of bread, it was risky. She'd be severely punished if caught.

"I was especially aware of the very rigid rule of no speaking. If we were lined up and moved or looked somewhere, we were punished. We had to be just as they wanted us, like a statue. No smiling, no talking. Silence. Life at the school meant no tenderness, no kindness. I was a lost little girl there. And I thought about home a lot, wondering why I had to be where I was, and why my parents had let me go. Later I learned they would have been jailed if they hadn't let me be taken."

And through it all at the St. Joseph's Mission School, the message was that anything and everything Indigenous was inferior, revolting even—whether it was their hair, their clothes, their language, their beliefs, their customs or their way of life. If it wasn't "white," if it wasn't Christian, it wasn't good. Impressionable children were methodically and comprehensively taught one thing: to be ashamed of themselves.

Phyllis reports that the abuse heaped upon children—emotional, physical and sexual—took some of them to early graves, either at the school or afterward, and adds that the word *genocide* doesn't cover what took place for over a century.

"Except for not being able to speak our language, I hadn't been told beforehand about the awful things that went on at mission schools," says Phyllis. "But I did hear about them from other students. At first, because I'd been raised to honour the church, the priests and the nuns through my mom and grandma, I didn't believe what was said. Priests and nuns surely wouldn't do such cruel things. I figured stories were being made up. That changed once I was there for a while. I watched how the priests and nuns treated the students and saw that they weren't who I thought they were. They were really mean. They were abusive and showed no respect for children.

And the rigid, very rigid life we had there was tearing apart what I thought was real. I'd always believed in priests and nuns, but slowly the truth came out. And in time, I also knew about the sexual abuse.

"When I was eleven or twelve years of age and started working with the old Oblates there, taking them food, I was subjected to sexual assault. I had to go to the room of one of them with food, and he would grab me, dragging me towards him. He would pull my hand and put it on his crotch, rubbing my hand on him. I'd struggle and get away from him. I knew that was so wrong! He was supposed to be a holy man. To me, he was the devil. I was scared of him, afraid to look him in the eye, and I knew he was a very bad man. It happened every time I had to deliver food to him.

"Another girl told me the same thing happened to her. So I knew I wasn't the only one. But I was anxious to change chores even though I knew I'd probably end up on kitchen duty again. I detested that old guy. He was so creepy.

"I only told one or two friends what was happening. No adults or authorities would have believed anything I'd say, and they probably would have punished me. They'd have blamed me."

To add to Phyllis's trauma, when that old priest died, the entire school, including those he abused, had to attend his funeral and listen to how he was such a fine person, a dedicated Oblate brother—accolades for a man who sexually abused children.

"I heard from older girls that priests were taking girls to their rooms. Priests were not supposed to do such things or be such persons. But I soon learned the stories were true when one of the students had a baby at the school. It was said she gave birth alone."

Phyllis was never able to tell anyone about the dreadful things that went on at school, not even her mother. Although Lily had attended residential school herself and undoubtedly learned, as Phyllis had, about the abhorrent behaviour of many of the staff, the fear and humiliation around such disclosure or discussion perpetuated the "don't tell" situation.

In fact, something happened to Phyllis at the mission that was so repulsive, so vile, that she vowed she would tell no one, ever—and never has. But she has been forced to live with it her entire life.

"Little Sister" was also left with triggers that always took her back to the dark days at residential school. "Men touching my hands, angry yelling, fighting—those things scared me for many years," Phyllis recalls. "Kids were maimed for life at that school, and nothing ever happened to the priests. No one was ever questioned. Parents didn't know what took place. Nothing was ever done about the abuse."

Phyllis was spared the nightmares that many children experienced during and after residential school. "I was so tired from all the work I did that I slept at the mission," she reports. "And when I was at home, I felt safe with Mom and Dad."

Phyllis soon learned how to protect herself at school. She conformed. Did what she was told to do. She didn't mingle much with the other kids but instead would go somewhere quiet to read when she had time, staying out of the way. In addition to the risk of sexual abuse, the dysfunction at residential schools resulted in children picking on each other, bullying one another. Phyllis wanted no part of that and mostly withdrew into herself.

The light within the little girl was snuffed out, her spark diminished—but one day it would reignite brighter than ever.

THE TRAUMA OF AN
EDUCATION IN DEFEATISM

HELPLESSNESS AND FRUSTRATION CAN DRIVE PEOPLE TO SELF-harm, sometimes into a pit with no bottom other than an end to life. Andy says he saw a lot of this growing up, but he somehow managed to outlast such sadness and grief.

"All the kids, especially the young ones, at residential school were simply sexual toys for the priests and supervisors," Andy says. "I had eight years in a prison for most of every year. Once, I was forced to eat a can of snuff, an entire can of crushed tobacco, while the priest laughed. How do you forgive that? My hate did not go away when I left. They stole *everything* from me."

Residential school robbed Andy of family, of a carefree childhood, of his language, of traditional Indigenous ways. Most of all, it annihilated his sense of self. All Andy heard through those horrific years was that everything about him, about his people, was detestable. The ongoing message had been that "things Indian" had to be changed. By the end of it, there was little left of the happy, confident boy who had entered residential school. The sixteen-year-old Andy was mostly angry.

"After residential school, as long as I was around my family and my people, I was pretty much okay," he says. "But as soon as someone from the mission came by, I felt automatic hatred. It was an instant flashback."

Sometimes an offhand remark, a callous "guy" joke or a racist comment would trigger an immediate return to what Andy called hell on earth. Something would conjure up a mental image that hurt him all over again, that outraged him all over again.

To ease those difficult flashbacks, Andy drank. On the weekends everyone around him also seemed to be into the poisonous legacy. Alcohol was introduced to the area's people in the 1940s and their dependency on it was not surprising given that multiple generations had been subjected to twisted residential school environments.

"I was angry at everything and everyone when I was drinking. But it dulled the pain, even though I didn't really like drinking," he says. "So much of our culture was lost—people were lost. I created my own world to some extent, my own view of things. I didn't want anyone interfering—I'd had enough of people telling me what to do during the years at the mission school. I didn't want anyone telling me what to do at home. And if they did, my reaction right away was antagonistic."

* * *

As it was with Andy, very little of what Phyllis learned at St. Joseph's Mission School was positive, nor was much of it of use to her as an adult, beyond basic household duties, learning to read and write English and some rudimentary arithmetic. In fact, the subsequent despondency and despair incapacitated her, haunted her, for decades.

Her belief in the goodness of priests and nuns was destroyed, as well as her belief in the Catholic church. Faith in the precepts of "white" religion was completely eroded—in stark contrast to the religious fervour of her mom and grandma.

Fortunately, there was a "bonding in hurt" that occurred at the mission. Phyllis developed a few friendships with girls she knew she could trust. "To this day, I have true friends from that school," she says. "Spending time with them when possible and going home, getting away from St. Joseph's, were the only good things I can remember about residential school. There was definitely no one in authority who treated me well."

Those in control at the school convinced Phyllis that all she had learned, known and loved during her young life was wrong. Her Indigenousness would commit her to the fires of hell unless she denounced it, gave it up. "The negative message I received was that I was not good enough," she says, "that my parents, my grandparents, my people were shameful and poor. All that is enough to make you pull away from a lot of things, from others. It's still like that for all of us today."

Such forced alienation from one's history and culture can result in isolation and detachment. On a personal level, Phyllis lost the ability to trust people beyond some of her immediate family. Retreating when confronted with new people, new places or new situations became her pattern.

Phyllis's withdrawal was also caused by the hurtful behaviour of other children at the mission school. "The rivalry and mean-spirited actions that happened are rarely spoken of," she says. "Kids bullied other kids. Old hurts, family disagreements and band issues were often acted out at the school. The aggressors would demand a share of whatever you had. If parents sent some candies or a bit of money, there would be someone who would want part or all of it. I learned to stay out of their way, to keep to myself. The priests and nuns seldom intervened—and if they did, they would punish both the kids, the bully and the victim."

According to Phyllis, this dark history remains largely unreported because the young people involved grew up, left residential school, often moved back to the same reserve or area and somehow had to learn to function within the same community—had to live with the grim ghosts of the past. Collective trauma leads to collective silence.

The estrangement from her family over many years created a surreal situation for Phyllis. "When I was allowed to be at home for summers and Christmas holidays, I had rather mixed feelings about the people there—they were my parents, but I didn't know them after being away from them for so long," she says. "It took finally leaving residential school and getting back to my former life to develop those relationships again. I had to work back to that. Some residential school students never achieved that, lost those connections altogether. And through it all, the question I could never ask was 'Why did you let them take me, Mom?' It was too hard. And I was the child."

After residential school, Phyllis attended Prince George Catholic High School, three hundred kilometres from her family. "I was boarded with a pleasant landlady but racism was rampant at that school," she says. "There were about thirty First Nations kids in my class. The teaching was shoddy and the education very poor. Students functioned mostly under fear just like at residential school. The atmosphere was one of intimidation.

"Discipline meant being strapped. The priest was strongest at the beginning of strapping but tired by the end. So First Nations kids were lined up at the head of the line, with non-Natives behind. Those hit first were struck really hard. One day I was fourth in line and my hands were so sore and swollen after the strapping that I couldn't hold cutlery to eat my lunch."

Phyllis would leave this replica of St. Joseph's Mission School during grade eleven. "Andy didn't have to attend that school. And I'm glad," she says. "The emotional cost of being away from family was the most difficult part. They were my parents, that was my home, but I didn't feel that or know that for sure, because I was away at school for years and years. I felt as though I didn't belong anymore, that I wasn't worthy of those people. I was given away, grew up without them. Yes, I eventually came home, but the sense of loss never left me."

When asked about the trauma that remained with her, about self-loathing, the hatred towards that molesting priest and others, the confusion, loss of culture, loss of language and no outlet for the anger, Phyllis did not speak. There was a long, silent pause. And then she cried. After fifty-seven years, what had happened to Phyllis could only be measured in her tears, could still induce deep grief.

THERE BE HORSES

ONE SMALL BRIGHT LIGHT SHONE FOR ANDY DURING THE trauma of residential school and being far from family for much of so many years—training and riding horses, all of which led to rodeoing during his teen years. By about age fourteen, Andy was taking part in the Alkali Lake "jackpot rodeo." Over his five decades of rodeoing, he would compete in the bareback, saddle bronc, calf roping and team roping competitions.

"Breaking and gentling a horse isn't that big a deal," he says. "I understand them well. And all animals tend to accept you after a while. I usually sense what a horse is all about, his temperament, what he's going to do, how he wants to be dealt with. I halter break them first and get them used to being handled, then start putting weight on their back and finally the saddle. Everything begins to fall in place as you work with them.

"We competed mostly on reserves but didn't get to too many [rodeos] when we were younger. No one had vehicles. So wherever we could get to on horseback is where we took part. Entries didn't close until an hour before the rodeo so there was time to get there.

"I didn't expect to do much more than compete. Didn't expect to win all the time. It was more about the camaraderie we shared there."

When asked if he was ever injured, Andy replies with a smile, "No, not seriously—I knew how to land!"

After competing for over ten years, Andy took a break from the local rodeo circuit in the late 1960s. Drinking was pervasive in his life, including after rodeo competitions. He was grappling with a fiend without hooves, struggling against a mean bronco with no bridle or reins—but he rode it to a standstill.

"Sobriety happened for me," he says, "and I started rodeo-ing again in the 1970s. Kept at it until about 2007 and retired not that long ago. I was doing team roping in the last years and had a roping arena at my place."

That he is still competing at age sixty-five says it all about Andy: strength, perseverance, challenging himself—and winning.

He passed on his love of horses and riding to three of his children. Ivy, Dean and Robert all learned to ride at a young age—and loved it. Robert would eventually help his dad at team roping events. Only one thing was better than spending time with their father, and that was time with Dad as well as a horse!

In the mid-1980s, Andy and a few of his rodeo friends formed the Alkali Roping Club, which ran for a number of years and provided members with practice space and time, as well as companionship around their sport—team building at its best.

Following residential school and its harmful environment, Phyllis also turned to horseback riding for comfort—not surprisingly, as both her family and Andy's were "horse people."

"When I was released from the mission school, I did some child care and homemaking for a couple of families," she says.

"But being out on the range, riding and cowboying were especially good for me. Got me out in nature and took me back to happy times up meadow when my family rode and roped."

Andy and Phyllis owned and loved horses for most of their years together.

Another aspect of "horsing around" involved the fifties and sixties movies that Andy, Phyllis and many of their friends often took in, and the glaring imbalance that played out in those spaghetti westerns wasn't lost on them. In the "cowboys and Indians" plots, during the confrontations the whites always won.

"We knew it was just a movie and often laughed about it, the false way it portrayed us," recalls Phyllis. "It wasn't anything major back then. We weren't speaking out about it yet. We knew how we lived, how it was, how we treated one another. And we also knew that, at that time, everyone bowed down to white people, that whites were seen to be right in everything, especially by the older generation, by our parents. But we young people were starting to question all that."

LIFE BACK ON THE REZ

MUCH HAD CHANGED AT THE RESERVE BY THE TIME ANDY returned. And the most detrimental change was that families could no longer "go up meadow." As previously described, the surrounding meadows had been where Alkali Lake's Esk'etemc family groups spent most of each year to escape the government-ordered constraints of living on the reserve.

Time there, in large natural fields, was taken up with haying, trapping, fishing, hunting and berry picking—a return to the land, to bygone days, to a time before "the white man." Old-time cabins, some of them log, some with sod roofs, became homesteads. Parents put in gardens. Kids learned to ride, to hunt and to fish and pitched in to help with family tasks. Even chores were fun.

But then the kids were gone, sent to residential school. Meadow life became unsustainable, for, as Andy relates, with the children leaving and subsequent loss of family allowance support, livestock often had to be sold. Soon there were no horses to hunt with. The life the people had known ended. And with that, Esk'etemc culture nearly vanished. It would ultimately be revived, but by the 1960s, spiritual and cultural activities at Alkali Lake were languishing from the multi-faceted, pervasive damage inflicted by colonization.

Andy saw all this. "As a teenager, I started working for different ranches, going from cow camp to cow camp. I became one of those guys who was a loner," he says. "I lived in camps and moved with the cattle, wherever work was happening. I worked like that, cowboying, for eight years. Like my dad. And Dad was often with me at that time. I kept learning more about horses, about the land and about livestock from him.

"After residential school, I found it hard to bond with people other than close family. I was quiet, didn't want to talk much or to too many people. Part of me just closed up. It was hard for me to trust still is."

That sense of personal isolation was surely exacerbated by the "code of silence" around residential school experiences, something that prevailed on reserves for many years. Andy says it was simply too difficult to speak of, and few listening would have believed the stories if they hadn't been there themselves. Talking about the brutality would cause it to exist vividly once again, would allow it to re-enter one's day-to-day living.

* * *

Being done with residential school definitely had its upside, but also its downside when Indigenous children left behind their years of confinement. Phyllis says returning to changed communities, new residences and relatives who didn't really feel like family anymore presented major challenges for young people who had been abused and degraded for up to ten years at mission schools.

For First Nations peoples, having to leave life up meadow and the introduction of alcohol and government welfare wrought huge transformations within their villages—none of them good. And the reserve restrictions felt very much like the constraints at residential school, Phyllis attests. "What we saw when we came home from school, the change in our parents because of alcohol, definitely wasn't good," she says. "Once social assistance was being paid, my parents moved to the reserve, and things went downhill from there. But then, the whole rez seemed to be in bad shape."

And one of the worst things for her upon returning was her family's immersion and belief in Catholicism—the religion that had done her so much harm, that had demeaned Little Sister to the point that she no longer existed. What Phyllis had once been had been buried under a mountain of hurt.

"I attended Mass regularly because my mom expected me to be there," she says. "But I wanted no part of it and eventually refused to go. I knew that the church and all its ritual was a mockery.

"It was a bit like being suspended between two worlds when I was at the mission for so much of each year. And I was a bit lost when school was over, but at least I knew I had some options, that I could find some kind of work."

Phyllis did find work, as a live-in homemaker and babysitter. "At that time, I did not feel part of the community because I was working and living elsewhere," she relates. "But part of me enjoyed being away, making my own way in the world and learning. Independence was good for me. And as I've said, I really liked cowboying some of that time."

Reconnecting with her former life was made more difficult by alcohol. A relative gave Phyllis her first drink when she was about seven or eight years of age. "It was a social thing," she says. "When we'd be back during the summer, it was the thing to do. And it helped us forget, helped erase some of the memories from residential school—at least for a while.

"I knew it was wrong, but everyone drank. It didn't seem wrong according to the adults, the parents and the leaders because they were all supplying. They were part of it. Most of them had ghosts from residential school that they were running from—they too needed to numb the pain. And the alcohol did not help with the attempts to rebond with family. It just made it harder. Misunderstandings happened. We only dealt with the surface of things, never getting to the bottom of what we really felt, of what had been done to us. That kind of necessary talk never happened when drink was involved."

Both Phyllis's siblings also had problems after residential school. "We'd been separated at the mission," she says. "We'd become detached, and we coped separately. The only time something would sort of come out was when we were drinking. It wasn't until we sobered up that we learned to listen to one another, to really talk ... and became close again."

Soon they realized that they were not the problem. The Chelseas started to understand that the system and the cruelty had been the problem. The loss of family, self-esteem, culture, language and links to the land made life more than difficult to manage after they were released from St. Joseph's Mission—released to somehow find their way again after the morass of residential school.

MARRIAGE, CHILDREN
AND STILL HURTING

DESPITE ALL HIS HURT, HIS SENSE OF NEEDING NO ONE, ANDY eventually married. Although he didn't know it at the time, his marriage to Phyllis Squinahan would bring with it life-altering change for both of them.

But at the beginning, their relationship stemmed from a friendship that started at St. Joseph's Mission School. Despite the reticence and timidity that developed during her residential school years, Phyllis felt she'd met a kindred spirit in a tall, good-looking young man she'd seen at St. Joseph's, and who was part of the group of young people who hung out together at the reserve in the early 1960s.

"Somehow Andy and I were okay interacting with each other, chatting and getting to know one another," she remembers. "I was shy and he was too, but we connected, laughed and talked when we'd run into each other at gatherings. There were films shown at the reserve on weekends—the projector was operated by a generator. It cost one dollar to see a movie, and it was a big event that everyone would try to attend.

"I think that even without speaking of school and its struggles, we knew we shared something, something that was dark. I remember feeling that I needed to be open to him. He was someone who was picked on at school and was left with problems. We both knew we didn't want to be like those terrible people there. And our friendship developed from that. I don't know why he wanted to talk with me, but somehow he recognized that I was receptive and was okay with that. Pretty soon we were special to each other."

Their relationship continued to deepen, and in 1964, Phyllis, aged twenty-one, and Andy, nearly twenty-two, were married, ironically, by a priest. "That was tough," says Phyllis, "but that's the way it had to be. And there was no Native culture as part of our ceremony."

All those attending their wedding had been drinking and were in a party mood. But beyond the bravado, Phyllis and Andy knew that they shared more than one bond and that they cared deeply for each other. Both their families of origin had been horse lovers and came from the same reserve. The two couples who were their parents had been friends as well. The other common denominator between Phyllis and Andy was language. Speaking the same dialect allowed them to talk comfortably about things, to understand thoroughly and to learn from and about each other, further cementing their connection.

However, the goodness they wanted within their marriage would be hampered by alcohol—and it had started with a lot of booze at the party after their wedding. "I was the only one who stayed sober," Phyllis recalls.

During their first year as husband and wife, they moved to Linde's Mill, a sawmill site founded in 1952 by the three

American Linde brothers, located about twenty-five kilometres from the reserve. Andy would work and the family would live there for thirteen years. Accommodation for workers' families consisted of simple cabins, but the Chelseas were together and that was all that mattered. Much like his father, Andy was a hard worker and a good provider. But the marriage existed under a pall of hurt and wounds—which would rear its dreadful head within the cloud of weekend alcohol binges.

Three children would be born during their time at the mill. "Ivy, Dean and Robert were our world," Phyllis says. "We were so happy to love and care for our kids. A wonderful bond formed. We were creating the family that had been ruined by residential school, creating family that we'd missed for so long."

For recreation at Linde's Mill, Andy pursued his second-favourite pastime after horseback riding. Hockey was an important sport for him even after residential school, where he had first skated. His dad, Patrick, was an avid hockey fan too, playing and coaching teams for years. Andy would eventually pass on this love of time on the ice to his children, and besides playing, he eventually organized a community hockey program at Alkali Lake.

"My days were predictable at the mill," says Phyllis, "getting up, having breakfast, Andy going off to work, house chores. And Andy always came home for lunch. My afternoons would often be spent doing laundry. And the kids played as kids do."

Phyllis recalls that she and Andy always shared the workload at home, and that Andy took full responsibility for their well-being and providing for them. "He even did diaper duty and helped with the kids when he came home," she recalls with a smile.

Watching their children grow, take their first steps, learn language and enjoy new things was all part of the fun of parenting—as were visits to relatives. It was of great benefit to family operations when they were finally able to purchase a car during their sawmill days.

"During the workweek, we were simply family, doing the day-to-day things that were part of family life," Phyllis says. "But getting together with friends was a whole other situation. That's when alcohol was involved and things would get rough. A different side of people would come out, and mostly it wasn't good."

She recalls that often the men wanted time together, but they didn't want the women visiting each other. "This created problems within families," she says. "It may have been a bit of a control issue around the men wanting to know what their women were up to. The women seemed to feel that their socializing wasn't acceptable to the guys, and so it rarely happened. There was resentment around that. We were all learning how to work within a relationship in a way that was fair, and lots of changes were happening with the arrival of children. Still, I missed the friends that I'd grown up with, those I'd known as girls. They weren't at Linde's Mill."

Phyllis adds, "Men would bring up personal things or make off-colour remarks. Alcohol definitely loosened tongues. Feelings would get bruised and sometimes a lot more than feelings. But you know, when I drank, I didn't have all the bad memories on my mind. I'd try to drink them out and wait. But they never really ever left me."

And so it was that weekends of less work and more free time meant drinking (although not for Phyllis during pregnancy).

Everyone they knew liked to, needed to, party hard. It was while drinking that Andy's unresolved anger from his brutal residential school days would present itself. The real Andy, the real Qluwenk, would be lost to hostile Andy, the bullied little boy who'd had no outlet for his fury.

Phyllis often bore the brunt of his lashing out, verbally and physically, but given her own negative experiences at mission school, she realized where it all originated. And through the rough patches, she was able to forgive, to let it go and to carry on. "He often hit me when he was drunk," she says with downcast eyes, "but never when he was sober. I had to put it behind me for the good of the family. I knew that wasn't the real Andy. It was the past, the brutality, the open wounds not healed."

She adds, "He knew that I knew where it all came from. It was terrible but I understood. We'd seen and experienced the harshness and the hard times at school, and related to each other in that way. We had that in common and we faced our difficulties. Andy and I recognized that our lives were not nearly as hard as the day we were taken from our parents or when we were so lonely at St. Joseph's. We got past it. We stayed together and worked through things. Never would have made it otherwise."

Many of the couple's problems arose from all that was hidden, they report—all that was left unspoken about the years of neglect and abuse. Given what was done to both male and female students by the residential school's priests and nuns, their ability to relate to the opposite sex and to function within intimate adult relationships had been terribly compromised, Phyllis says. Without counselling to help them recover, they had almost no concept of what constituted normal behaviour.

The abuse Phyllis had suffered at residential school affected her ability to discuss sexual matters with her children later in life. "I just couldn't go there," she says. "It was so difficult for me. And it was the same for most residential school Survivors. But it's different today. We have workshops and discussions when we talk about such things, for both men and women. There is a way to think things through and talk them through. It's now okay to give voice to it. And some just come and listen and learn. At least they know they're not alone in what they feel and think."

Phyllis and Andy never allowed the hard times to consume either their marriage or their family. It proved to be an obscure blessing that they completely understood the source of their respective struggles, that they were able to hold on to each other when the painful past threatened to overwhelm them.

Even before they could actually talk about the horrors of mission school, the couple were able to relate to each other, each innately understanding where the other was coming from—and this would ultimately save them, would allow them to go on to bigger and better things personally and professionally. As Andy says, they never would have made it if they hadn't gone through similar hardships.

A CHILD SPEAKS AND NEW
FRIENDSHIPS FORM

BY 1971, UNBEKNOWNST TO ANDY AND PHYLLIS, GREAT CHANGE
was in the air, bringing with it a transformation that would
spread far beyond their family.

The family had moved from Linde's Mill back to the reserve,
where sons Kevin and Owen were born. Always industrious,
Andy was soon managing his own logging company.

Their home life continued as it had been. However, being
on the reserve again reminded them of living at the mission
school. Freedom was curtailed, decisions were confined to
what the Department of Indian Affairs allowed, and Chief and
council were in control. Phyllis and Andy report that it was
residential school with another name, but with one exception:
given the established patterns, socializing and weekend partying
continued to involve drinking.

Introduced to Indigenous people in the area during the
1940s, alcohol had become integral to getting together on the
reserve, as it had been at Linde's Mill. Difficulties with grocery
stores near the reserve led to the Chelseas opening a store that
sold supplies at their home on the reserve to serve locals. In

time, the shop would have its own location, but it started in the Chelsea basement.

When Phyllis and Andy were with their friends during weekends, Grandma Lily (Phyllis's mother) often looked after the Chelsea children. And it was following such a weekend that Phyllis would be forced to recognize and comprehend the problems she and Andy had foisted upon their kids.

"I arrived at my mom's to pick up the children," Phyllis recalls, "and seven-year-old Ivy, our oldest, stated emphatically that she was not coming home with me because her dad and I drank too much. She said she was staying with her Kyé7e, her grandma, as were her younger brothers. My children were refusing to live with us! And I knew my mom would keep the kids with her if that happened.

"I went home alone, in a state of shock. I was losing my children because of booze. And I realized I would be repeating what had happened to me when our parents gave us away, let us be taken to residential school. I would be doing the same thing— my kids would feel the same way I did—if I didn't change. I knew what I had to do and made that choice. Didn't speak to anyone about it, just set my mind to it. I felt really alone in that decision, but my drinking had to stop immediately.

"Andy arrived home soon after I did, and I told him that Ivy didn't want to come home because we drank too much, that she wanted to live with her grandmother. Without discussion, I told Andy right then that I was going to pick up the kids, and did. I knew I was finished with alcohol."

Within a week, Andy had given up drinking too. He came home, was sitting with the family and quickly said, "I'm going to quit drinking too." And that was that.

Phyllis was greatly relieved. "There was a lot of uncertainty and fear for me during that week. I didn't know what would happen. Things might not go well at all. If Andy came home after drinking, he might beat me—he could be really mean when he drank. Or I might have to leave. Andy would never leave his kids, and if things became worse, I would have to be the one to go. Didn't want to lose my kids because of drinking, and I certainly didn't want to have to leave the family because I'd stopped drinking."

Andy deeply regrets the misery he caused his wife and family because of the unresolved childhood anger unleashed by alcohol. "It all threatened our marriage many times, but we managed to survive it," he says.

"You know, I never really liked drinking in the first place. It was a symptom of a deeper hurt. That's all it was, something to bury what happened at St. Joseph's Mission, even if for a while. And boozing was the thing to do, to go along with what everyone else was doing. It was just part of fitting in socially. So it wasn't that hard for me to give it up. My granny would have been glad that it came to an end."

Both Phyllis and Andy agree that the changes within their family and as a couple at that time were drastic—and all positive. Everything got better. Giving up alcohol resulted in their being less angry, less hurt and more aware of all the good between them.

* * *

Soon after this momentous shift in their lifestyle, three significant people came into Phyllis and Andy's lives: Diana French,

Alan Haig-Brown and Lorne Dufour provided support and encouragement, and in the process, became lifelong friends of the Chelseas.

Diana, a reporter by profession, also served as a trustee on the local school board, as did Phyllis, in the mid-1970s. An important initiative at that time was the first Indian Education Program, which introduced Indigenous language and cultural components to school curricula on reserves. Phyllis was a driving force behind this for her community's school, where Alan was principal. Implementation of the new and essential subject matter was something they all championed.

"I was working with a man who cared about the kids the way I did," Phyllis says of Alan. "It was all about the students. Alan's wife was First Nations so he was particularly aware of what was needed to provide a more complete education for Indigenous children. We value and have always valued his opinion, professionally and as a close friend."

Lorne was a hard-working teacher at the Alkali Lake school—an especially dedicated teacher who instilled cultural and personal pride in his students. He taught the Chelsea children and befriended their parents. He recalls, "It was the love Phyllis and Andy shared that kept everyone together in the seventies." Lorne would eventually write *Jacob's Prayer*, a book that tells the moving story of his time with the Esk'etemc of Alkali Lake.

Diana first met Andy when she was reporting for the *Williams Lake Tribune* on First Nations topics. "Even before he was Chief, Andy was an outspoken community leader who did not mince words about what needed improvement on-reserve, what would make it a better place for people, about what was fair," Diana says. "He fought for his band on many fronts, and his compassion was at the bottom of it all."

Phyllis, Andy and Diana became good friends. The Chelsea family would stay in Williams Lake at Diana and husband Bob's residence if things on the reserve became overheated—such as during the time Andy and Phyllis were putting in place preventive measures to help their friends and family overcome the alcohol dependence resulting from psychological and physical impairment they'd suffered over the years. And daughter Ivy stayed with the Frenches during her grade twelve school year.

"Our friendship was and is reciprocal," Diana says. "I got a lot from the relationship too, not the least of which was enjoying the off-the-wall sense of humour that Andy and Phyllis possess. It catches you unawares at times but it's always effective and funny."

During the 1970s, '80s and '90s, the Chelseas' path would often cross that of another significant person—Sage Birchwater. A back-to-the-lander who lived on a trapline outside Williams Lake for twenty-four of his forty-four years in the area, Sage was subsequently retained as a journalist for the *Williams Lake Tribune* in 2001 and would often cover stories on the Esk'et First Nation.

"Beyond the media reporting, I so admired what the Chelseas undertook, was so impressed by the motivation displayed by their entire community," Sage says. "Phyllis and Andy had to deal with isolation when they gave up alcohol. Their intensity and courage was impressive. You know, alcohol creates wastelands, but following the example of the Chelseas, the Alkali Lake band retrieved a wasteland and rebuilt a village, literally and figuratively."

Sage would evolve from his journalistic role to become a knowledgeable folklorist and would write or co-write numerous books about the people and places of the Cariboo-Chilcotin area in British Columbia's Central Interior.

"I was so taken with the vastness of the area around Williams Lake," he says. "It drew me and I lived within it for over twenty-five years. Over that time, I so enjoyed running into Andy, and sometimes Phyllis, in town, and our subsequent chats. My work with the town's Friendship Centre brought us together as well. They were an amazing team. There was a magic about them."

And so the alchemy of the Chelseas touched yet another person. Theirs was an almost mystical strength that drew people to them, that sustained them when all seemed black and difficult. To their family, friends and neighbours, it would prove to be an extraordinary gift.

SPIRITUALITY, BELIEFS AND CULTURE WITHIN THE CHELSEA FAMILY

IN THE FEW YEARS ANDY AND PHYLLIS ENJOYED AS CHILDREN before being taken to residential school, they thoroughly absorbed the teachings and spirituality of their grandparents and parents—and that wisdom never left them. They at no time gave up the innate belief in their ability to be who they truly were. Beatings and abuse, though damaging, did not destroy them entirely.

For Andy, no matter what was done to him on the outside, it never diminished his strength inside. "I wouldn't let that happen," he says firmly. "I wasn't going to let them change who I really was regardless of the abuse." And he never felt inadequate, even when he was browbeaten physically and emotionally. Andy held on to what he'd been taught: all are equal on this planet.

His family had instilled in him something unfaltering—his power. And he never gave that away. "I wouldn't let anyone get the best of me," he says.

"For me," says Phyllis, "in the midst of all the turmoil and hurt at the mission school, I needed to hold on to what was deep within myself, to come from the place of a person who loved her dad, had a grandma and valued family. I was Secwepemc and never forgot that. It remained with me. Those things kept me solid and sane at residential school. And I've preserved them all my life. Could never be taken from me; they were all part of me. Andy and I believed in that same spirit."

Andy and Phyllis were able to reclaim their family's culture during the two months of summer when they returned home from school. Familiar habits surrounded them and familiar places welcomed them. "We were Secwepemc people living our ways, living off the land, riding, cowboying and speaking our language with Elders—reconnecting with relatives and honouring our lifestyle," says Phyllis.

Their families had made use of Sweat Lodges, and their fathers, neither of whom had been confined to residential school, believed in their First Nation's culture, using long-standing rituals when hunting, fishing or working in the bush. It was the way to be, the way to pay tribute to all. They belonged there, connected to their land.

It was the Chelseas' belief that the Creator had given them the sacrosanct duty to protect the land, its forests, the air and water and the life therein, and that their rights emanated from their relationship to the land, which is a living, breathing entity. Mother Earth would look after them in all ways, if they looked after Mother Earth.

Traditional ways came from honour. And to their children, Phyllis and Andy passed on that respect for and connectedness to the land; it was their responsibility. Trees, rocks, water and animals were more than trees, rocks, water and animals. Venerating the Sweat Lodge, food offerings, smudging and animals were integral to acknowledging the ways of their ancestors and accepting the obligations conveyed to them by the Creator.

Phyllis and Andy wanted their kids to grow up adapting Secwepemc culture to modernity, integrating it with their way of living. As individuals, their children would have distinct choices. They would have to decide how they would carry themselves through life.

"There are many influences that pull kids in various directions," Phyllis says. "As teenagers, social life is important to them. All teens everywhere want to fit in. And sometimes it can be their undoing. Then, as adults, they have to choose what works for them. All parents can do is love them."

And part of that loving meant instilling recognition of Secwepemc values, the basis of a wholesome outlook and a healthy life within their ethnicity. The importance of relationships was stressed—connection to others and to the natural world around them. Nurturing individual strengths and responsibility was integral to their family and was ably demonstrated by Andy and Phyllis as they rebuilt their lives.

Through their parents and grandparents, the Chelsea children were encouraged to develop their personal gifts and to explore spirituality. Through stressful times and the pressures of day-to-day living, the family held on to the importance of celebration, of humour and of rest, as part of their collective restoration.

STARTING OVER AND
LEARNING TO LIVE AGAIN

FEELING OPTIMISTIC AND CONFIDENT IN THEIR RESOLUTION TO put alcohol behind them, Andy and Phyllis were, at last, able to talk meaningfully, were able to speak in earnest about the bad that had happened between them, and it helped. They learned to fully trust one another and to accept each other, despite what may have happened before abstinence. The past was over. They were embarking on a future that would be much changed—new beginnings were in front of them.

The major adjustment that occurred post-alcohol was that Phyllis and Andy began to wholly support each other in what they wanted to do. They made space for each of them to work in their areas of interest and allowed for time to be spent with their individual friends. They developed a solid belief in each other and created an environment in which they both could grow.

"We learned to share time beyond us," says Phyllis, "with our friends and with our work interests. Definitely a good thing."

Despite this, Andy and Phyllis realized they would be tested within their community. A decades-long habit of alcohol use interwoven into community life meant resistance was bound to arise.

"Basically, everyone on the rez hated us for not drinking," recalls Andy. "Even our own brothers and sisters. That was the hardest to bear. And it was lonely. When you're the only two non-drinkers in the community, you're not invited out much. All we could do was take it one day at a time and support each other."

Phyllis adds, "People we knew well begrudgingly allowed us to occasionally take part in whatever was going on and would claim they were going to quit drinking too, but it wasn't so at that time. It was as if they were pretending to be happy to see us. Andy and I had to learn how to mingle, how to fit in, sober."

Significantly, it wasn't just blood relatives who were "family" on the reserve. Such a tight-knit, small community meant they all felt like a large extended family. "We had to come together as a unit," says Phyllis. "That took individual work within each of us to not only learn to trust ourselves, but also trust in opening up to one another. Such interaction doesn't just happen because people have sobered up.

"Truly being with people on our rez helped make abstinence easier for me. I knew I had to come from a place of total acceptance of them and not back away from what needed to be said or dealt with, whether it was about their kids, their drinking or a beating, because I cared about them. And they needed to know that. That's how I went from day to day, reaching out, connecting."

"From the change in Phyllis and me," says Andy, "change started within the community, so we kept it going. People needed something else. They hated what was going on but didn't know how to pull themselves out of it."

Several years after the critical decision was made by Phyllis and Andy to embrace sobriety, they learned of a person who was connected to an Alcoholics Anonymous (AA) program in Williams Lake. Phyllis contacted Oblate brother Ed Lynch (now deceased), who was soon coming out to the reserve. When asked if it was difficult to have an Oblate brother involved with the Alkali Lake community in light of her residential school experience, Phyllis serves up one of her usual pragmatic replies: "I deal with people as people and don't put much stock in titles— and Ed was a pretty good guy."

Initially it was just Ed, Andy and Phyllis getting together in their living room. But gradually, starting with one of their friends, two or three people would attend. Soon they had to arrange a larger AA meeting place.

"In the beginning, we were just helping each other, communicating, and nothing further than that," relates Phyllis. "But as more people contacted us, asking about anti-alcohol programs, I learned there were resources that I hadn't explored. We'd been simply working at Alkali Lake, to do what seemed to help ourselves and others on the rez."

Phyllis learned that there were professional ways to do what she was doing from her heart. "As it was, we were doing the right things," she says, "but I undertook training on how to handle a variety of problems."

The coming together, the societal rebuilding process at Alkali Lake, would ultimately take years. But it happened. And the story of how it happened is one of courage, caring and fortitude.

REACHING OUT, LIFTING UP

GIVEN THE CLEAR EVIDENCE OF HARM CREATED BY RESIDENTIAL schools, it is mind-boggling that Canadian governments would embark on yet another program of separating Indigenous children from their families.

Andy and Phyllis were directly involved in protecting children of the Esk'et First Nation from being removed from their family homes: they intervened by taking action, always their go-to solution when facing injustice.

The term "Sixties Scoop" was coined by Patrick Johnston, a researcher with the Canadian Council on Social Development, in his 1983 book on Indigenous children in the child welfare system.[1] The term fittingly describes the reprehensible process of seizing Indigenous children that persisted from the 1960s through the 1980s. This, however, is a simplistic description of what took place. Regardless of the supposedly overarching goal of protecting First Nations children, the seizures were more of the same assimilative, integrationist, anti-Indigenous

---

1   Johnston, *Native Children and the Child Welfare System.*

policy propagated in the late nineteenth and early twentieth centuries.

The Scoop began administratively with amendments to the Indian Act in 1951 that assigned Indigenous child welfare jurisdiction to the provinces, with no additional financial support. Such authority had not existed federally or provincially prior to this questionable decision. However, the lead-up to the removal of Indigenous children began long before that. The federal government's underfunding of housing, resources, education and services on reserves fostered widespread poverty, high death rates and socio-economic barriers for those who lived there. Added to the pervasive racism and historic trauma of residential schools passed from generation to generation, this resulted in communities facing deep distress that has yet to be addressed and remedied within most Indigenous populations.[2]

Rather than demand federal support or provide additional resources to reserves, provincial child welfare agencies chose instead to remove children from their parents and their homes— shades of the assimilation policies of residential schools all over again, but with some horrific differences: children seized were not only placed with or adopted by non-Indigenous families but also sent abroad, some as far away as New Zealand. It is estimated that in 1981, approximately 50 percent of the Indigenous children seized in Canada ended up with families in the United States.

Additionally, child welfare departments did not require that social workers charged with assessing conditions in First

---

2   Edwards, "Fighting Foster Care"; Sinclair and Dainard, "Sixties Scoop."

Nations homes have any training or knowledge of Indigenous cultures, diet, familial structure or social mores—nor were they required to obtain communities' consent to take newborn and young children from parents. It wouldn't be until the 1980s that legislation would be enacted requiring social workers to notify Indigenous authorities of a child's removal from the community.[3]

Child welfare staff descending on poor Indigenous communities came with only Euro-Canadian concepts of what constituted acceptable domestic situations and available foodstuffs. Berries, fish, dried game and root vegetables found in a refrigerator were enough to justify seizing children, citing malnourishment. It would be lost on them that non-Indigenous foods were, firstly, either unavailable or far too expensive and, secondly, not what First Nations peoples were used to eating. The white flour, refined white sugar and salt introduced to Indigenous Peoples have been widely considered detrimental to their health.

It is estimated that more than twenty thousand First Nations, Métis and Inuit children were taken from their homes and placed in non-Indigenous care before a critical assessment of the consequences was made in the 1980s.

"We did our best not to let it happen," says Phyllis. "Andy and I regularly had a number of rez children living at our place to keep them from social workers who had showed up.

"And it was particularly significant to me to protect such children because of what happened when I was a teenager in the 1960s. One day back then, I was asked to translate for my aunt who was meeting with social services people. I was

3   Sinclair and Dainard, "Sixties Scoop."

completely unaware of what it was all about until the conversation was well on its way. They wanted to take my baby cousin away—and I had to deliver that hurtful message in our language to my aunt. Her infant daughter was in fact taken and never returned home. The damage was done, started that day, and was never repaired. I hated what had happened. Hated that I was part of it.

"Years later, we would first try to place children under threat of seizure with relatives, but if that wasn't possible, we just took them in. They'd stay with us for a few months and then return to their parents, who probably did not deserve to lose their kids in the first place. It was all about defeating an unfair system, a hurtful process that was often based on lies or misunderstanding of our way of life."

The enduring effects of the Sixties Scoop are wide-ranging. Perhaps the most significant is the state of limbo in which seized children found themselves, both as kids and adults—for they were no longer Indigenous and they were not "white." The low self-esteem, shame, loneliness, loss and confusion that arose, especially when adoptees learned later in life of their actual origins, can only be described as immensely frustrating and stressful emotionally.[4]

Even those children placed in loving and welcoming homes were not and could not be inculcated with culturally significant education and experiences to promote and nurture their Indigenous identities. And those who were victims of physical and/or sexual abuse in foster or adoptive families were damaged beyond belief.

---

4   Sinclair and Dainard, "Sixties Scoop."

Patrick Johnston's *Native Children and the Child Welfare System*, Judge Edwin Kimelman's 1985 report, *No Quiet Place*, and First Nations' ongoing demands that provincial adoption laws be revised finally brought about changes to child welfare policies. These efforts resulted in adoption priority being given to extended family first and then another Indigenous family before any child could be placed with a non-Indigenous household.

The disproportionately high number of Indigenous children in government care compared with the percentage of Indigenous Peoples within the general population has become an issue of great concern. In late 2018, the federal government announced that, in consultation with First Nations, Inuit and Métis, diligent work would commence in 2019 on new child welfare legislation to bring an end to the removal of Indigenous children from their homes, families and communities.

***

One of the most significant issues that Andy and Phyllis overcame was the culture around alcohol within the Esk'et community and elsewhere, which was "Don't trust, don't talk and don't feel." They broke down such barriers in a gentle way that led others to believe the Chelseas could be trusted—and through that, community members began to talk and once again discover emotion. Andy and Phyllis inadvertently became the catalyst that would lead to eradicating the poisonous code that had permeated their community.

During this time, Andy was presented with what seemed a preordained opportunity: he was appointed Chief of the Esk'et

First Nation when the Nation's first elected Chief resigned mid-term. Andy was asked to step in, and he, without doubt, stepped *up*, taking on responsibility for people he cared about and for a village in turmoil.

It was 1972—nearly twenty-five years since Andy's granny had taken him into the mountains to fast and had predicted he would one day be Chief of his people.

Phyllis wholly supported him in his decision. "I knew he needed to do that and that he'd be good at it. He was reaching outside the community to make changes, to bring in programs and to develop things that would help the band. Andy brought excellence and a take-no-prisoners attitude to those types of efforts. And he was respected."

Phyllis was the perfect mate as Andy took on the mantle of Chief. "Andy saw the big picture. He knew what needed to happen on the rez. But I was the one who could set up meetings, arrange attendees, draw up the agenda. And just ask him to be there. I was the organizer. Andy could drive issues."

Through the supportive process that developed, the couple continued to disclose matters that were important to them. "The best thing to come out of listening and learning is that every person is creating their own 'walk,' realizing they can trust themselves to just be themselves and to know that they are special," Phyllis says. "I walk that walk wherever I go, and I'm understanding more each time I do that."

Helping others on the reserve came from gradual beginnings. When Phyllis and Andy would hear of trouble that had occurred, usually over a weekend, they went to those who had been involved on Monday. "We dealt with it, rather than looking the other way," Phyllis says.

"People in the band hated what had been going on for years," says Andy. "They needed something to change but didn't know how to pull themselves out of it. The Monday get-togethers were mostly peaceful and didn't involve the police. We'd round up those who'd been part of the problem and sit down to talk with them. Didn't discuss what they'd done on the weekend or alcohol's part in it. We'd talk about what they wanted to do with their life, what they wanted out of life. There was no judgment, and we didn't tell them what to do.

"If violence had occurred, we'd get the parties together to talk, not to say there was something wrong with them. It's not that they hated each other. The problem was the alcohol, not them. We'd get them to discuss why they were drinking. Flashbacks to residential school occur when there's drinking, and then people can get angry about almost anything."

"If Andy helped a fellow trying to change things to find a job, we'd put him with someone who'd been sober for a while," adds Phyllis. "It was like having an AA meeting while they were working."

The other egregious problem was sexual abuse—both at residential school and within the community. Some who had been abused as children became abusers in adulthood. At the very least, the physical and sexual abuse meted out by St. Joseph's priests and nuns would have left their victims with an unhealthy imprint about sex. Eventually, with encouragement from Phyllis and Andy, the people of Alkali Lake were able to pull back the curtain on this obstruction to healthy relationships and examine it critically.

"We certainly talked about sexual abuse—in a big way," Andy says. "That type of thing didn't happen in the past. In our culture, we never, never abused the life givers. It goes right back to the arrival of white men."

Andy and Phyllis estimate that by the mid-1980s, 90 percent of Alkali Lake band members had been victims of physical and/ or sexual abuse—the result of the horrors of residential school and the subsequent abuse within families. And sadly, many had become what others called them, "the Indians of Alcohol Lake"—the majority dependent on social assistance payments that fuelled the vicious circle of drinking, abuse, sobering up temporarily and drinking again.

*　*　*

Early on at Alkali Lake, most of the self-help sessions were held without professionals, although occasionally a social worker or psychologist would be called in when needed. Get-togethers were mostly friend-to-friend gatherings. Problems were talked out. And soon, as part of their recovery, community members began to use the Sweat Lodges, the pipe, sacred herbs and smudging ceremonies that had been given up over many years. Time-honoured cultural practices were reinstated, with the First Nation reclaiming its dance, drumming and songs as part of its recovery. "No one but its citizens could help our community initially. It had to come from within. They had to choose change, had to want things to improve. And both these things happened," Andy says.

"One day, in 1985, we had 270 people lined up for discussions about the abuse, and the gathering went on from 9:00 a.m. to 3:00 a.m. the next night," Andy recalls. "Everyone had their say; everyone was able to talk about what had happened to them, without being judged. Let it all out. People agreed about what was done to us, also that we were now doing it to our own. And it wasn't right. This opened the gates for everyone to know what was done to others on the rez when they were drinking. Some didn't remember what had happened. Some did. And yet they still talked about it. It was a time of healing. And they made the decision to protect one another."

"We had five counsellors present," adds Phyllis, "to support those attending, but we basically ran it ourselves. There were teens to Elders as part of the group. We sat in a large circle and had a talking feather. Everyone spoke and no one left. Food was brought in. There was a respectful silence working within the whole crowd."

Hereditary Chief Irvine Johnson says, "I was there for all of it, and I think the most difficult part of it was that some people were 'outed,' but they had to be for others to heal, and in order that they could talk about it. Residential school caused the abuse, and it carried on afterward. It was awful. Some recovered and others never did. They just stayed with the 'bottle gun' to their head and perished."

Everything was discussed at that significant event, from personal childhood abuse to abuse after residential school and abusing others. Many of the men apologized to the women they had hurt. It was heart-wrenching and healing. Tears were shed and hugs were exchanged. Phyllis called it a day of miracles. And it was a day that needed to happen.

Ultimately, what developed was a multi-faceted, holistic method of approaching the subject, composed of the justice system, a healing process that included counselling, participation in a Survivors or abusers support group, and reconciliation between victims and abusers and their families.

As rebuilding progressed, Andy and Phyllis found they frequently had many people temporarily staying in their home, in addition to children they were sheltering from social services seizure. "Often it was people we didn't know, but they needed some place to be safe, to rest, to have meals—adults and their kids," says Phyllis. "There are a lot of rez kids alive today because we stood up for them and made changes. They're training for gainful employment; some will become nurses, doctors and lawyers. We gave them the option of imagining and choosing a different way of being. We simply did it because it had to be done, but to see the results is especially gratifying.

"However, as time went on back then, our children didn't like all those people being with us. They wanted our home to just be our home. So we arranged for space away from our residence—a place where people could get together and talk. We knew it had to happen when it needed to happen."

Willingly having others from outside their family dependent on them off and on meant that during his first years as Chief, Andy didn't have much money left over—and in fact, after twelve years as Chief and helping others, he was in the hole by almost $90,000. "My family understood—I spent money on everyone else except my family most of the time," he says with a rueful grin. "So I took a few years off from being Chief and started my own logging business. And at that time, Phyllis was employed by the school district for several years, as well as running the rez store. When we got out of debt, I decided to run for Chief again."

Andy Chelsea—Qluwenk—would serve as Chief of the Esk'etemc of Alkali Lake for a total of twenty-seven years, being re-elected every two years after his hiatus from that position.

Phyllis also contributed her time and talent on and off the reserve. "In addition to being a school trustee, I worked in the courts for about one year," she says. "Considered being a lawyer and would have been accepted at the University of Victoria, but we really didn't want to leave our home, the family and those others within the community who needed us." She adds with a smile, "Andy wouldn't have been very happy without his horses either."

Phyllis taught the first Shuswap Language Program in British Columbia at the Esk'et school. With crucial help from Diana French, she lobbied for and was successful in acquiring a coordinator for First Nations within the Cariboo-Chilcotin School District. Alan Haig-Brown would capably carry out that job for the next eleven years. And during that time, First Nations staff positions went from zero to nearly twenty. Full programs from kindergarten to grade twelve in the Secwepemctsín and Tsilhqot'in languages were developed, as well as in the Dakelh/Carrier language for grades one to ten. Area Indigenous Peoples were making important changes within their education system.

From 1972 to 1976, Phyllis would serve first as welfare aid and subsequently as social worker at Alkali Lake. Over many years, she and Andy would do all they did from the heart—because they cared. They knew the people, knew their ways, knew the words to say, knew what to do. And it worked.

COMMUNITY LEADERSHIP

BEGINS AT HOME

DESPITE THEIR WORK THROUGH ONE-TO-ONE COMFORT AND assistance, as well as the ongoing positive steps taken by many community members, Andy and Phyllis couldn't help but notice continuing pervasive struggles at the reserve. Alcohol was still running through the community, anger often overtook relationships, kids were sometimes unfed, houses were neglected, the local priest was a problem and people were dying far too young—in one year sixteen deaths within the community of several hundred were related to alcohol and the diseases it causes. Governments, priests, nuns, residential schools and Indian agents were culpable, were accessories to those deaths and dysfunction, but it would be the Survivors who would ultimately save themselves. No help would be forthcoming from the ones who caused and allowed the horrific loss of life and destruction of pride. But transformation was about to materialize.

By 1974, the band had taken over local school management and had a building constructed after petitioning the Department of Indian Affairs. "We hired our own teachers and the kids really liked being educated in their own community," Andy says. "Before that, we couldn't teach our language or our customs. And the curriculum was so far behind what was taught in Williams Lake. On the rez, it had been confined to religion, social studies and sciences, but we got that changed.

"We persevered—it took a lot of involved meetings and negotiations about courses, programs, budgets and responsibilities. But we steamrolled our ideas and in time were successful." With a smaller enrolment, the Alkali Lake school was still operating over forty years later.

Beginning with their vow of sobriety in 1971, Andy and Phyllis, supported by the band council, would implement changes that, although initially unpopular in the community, would prove to be the beginning of the last gasp of rampant alcoholism at the Alkali Lake reserve for decades.

Bootlegging was widespread. "Everyone did it," says Phyllis, "even Andy and I for a short while when we moved back to the reserve. And Chief and council at that time would drink with everyone. Alcohol was still given to kids. It was a way of living that had taken hold."

With the advent of social assistance in the mid-twentieth century, acquiring alcohol on a reserve became a much simpler proposition. Welfare money was quickly exchanged for a bottle. An increase in drinking problems ensued and bootleggers profited.

The next step would be to catch bootleggers in the act. Phyllis and Andy report that the Royal Canadian Mounted Police (RCMP) simply ignored bootlegging on the reserve. "It wasn't a concern for them—their friends and relatives weren't the ones dying," says Phyllis. "And turning a blind eye goes on to this day even in Williams Lake, whether bootlegging involves Native or non-Native people."

At that early stage of helping the village to rehabilitate, the Chelseas went to the RCMP and devised a plan that would involve marked bills to be used to buy alcohol from reserve bootleggers. Everyone knew who sold booze, but there had to be concrete proof. Marked money would be used for the purchases to be carried out by community members in on the plot. Those caught were to be threatened with legal repercussions but not formally charged. The authorities agreed and waited just outside the reserve, ready to be called into action.

"When we asked what cash was to be used, we were told the RCMP had no money for such a 'sting' operation," Phyllis says. "So I ended up using our money, which I never got back— it became evidence." The Chelseas personally provided the $60, which in 2019 would be the equivalent of around $375, not exactly small change.

Half a dozen bootleggers were scooped up that afternoon— and again, the Chelseas played no favourites. Both Andy's mother and Phyllis's were caught by the ruse. There were others still covertly selling alcohol on the reserve, but in such a small community, they were always found out. And then those booze vendors would get a visit from Chief Andy—and that usually persuaded them to change their ways for the good of the community.

The other vector for alcohol was a passenger and goods bus service called the Dog Creek Stage, which ran regularly between the community of Williams Lake, the Alkali Lake reserve and the Dog Creek First Nation. Its driver would collect money on one run and deliver liquor on the next. Andy put a stop to this soon after the sobriety efforts were underway—the stage would no longer be a convenient delivery method for what was poisoning the community.

And then there was the Roman Catholic priest on the reserve. This man of the cloth was also a man of the bottle—he was an alcoholic. In addition, he was involved romantically with the reserve nurse. Chief Andy was a leader who took action when and where it was needed. The corrupt priest was told by the forthright Chief to leave the community. And he left.

While these radical initiatives were being carried out, Andy sometimes felt an undercurrent of fear—not for himself but for his family, for the Chelseas were the "face" of what was happening. "However, those who were angry were people I knew well," he says. "A lot of the time, it was just verbal threats. It was the alcohol talking. And nothing ever did happen to any of us."

A treatment centre in Williams Lake was instrumental in helping the Alkali Lake reserve slough off its alcoholism. Many people would eventually seek help there. And when they returned to the reserve, they would find that friends and family had cleaned and repaired their homes. They were off to a fresh start in many aspects of their lives, and the very special "welcome home" projects that were undertaken did much to set them firmly on that new course.

The community's new way of living also included planning "dry" events and gatherings such as for New Year's, AA groups, monthly youth meetings and a 9:00 p.m. curfew for young people. "A curfew had to be put in place for a while," says Phyllis, "for parents to realize that their kids needed sleep, needed to follow a schedule. Band members soon took it on themselves as something that needed to happen within their families."

Andy regularly attended the youth get-togethers, Phyllis reports. "The kids there were open to saying what they wanted, and Andy as Chief was prepared to listen and to support them in that—whether it was to learn some of the old ways, to learn how to hunt or to form a dance group."

For the first ten to fifteen years of the intervention that Andy and Phyllis started, the work was carried out by the people themselves. Meetings with those needing assistance happened quickly—friends reaching out to friends, family reconnecting with family. They talked, they listened, they handled it themselves. It was a grassroots initiative that flourished from within.

Although they are thankful that a semblance of this exists today on reserves, Phyllis and Andy feel that the warmth and immediacy of past mediation has been lost in present-day action. Understandably, they say, the non-Indigenous professionals hired are unfamiliar with First Nations ways and community history, and are available only by appointment from nine to five on weekdays. Should troubles arise on weekends, the RCMP detachment is called. In addition, the judiciary often becomes involved—people may lose their children or be removed from the reserve. The Chelseas were all about preserving families, bonding with others and reaching out whenever needed. They lived this and conveyed it to those around them. But things have changed—rules and regulations dictate what happens now. If something goes awry, litigation can ensue. The former Chief and the social worker sense that the new ways of the new system, however, do not involve sensitivity or empathy.

* * *

In any dissertation about alcohol and Indigenous populations, it's important to point out that Indigenous people do not have a genetic predisposition to alcoholism. There is no evidence to support this. Some professionals on the subject contend that the introduction of rotgut intoxicants and the drunken conduct of European settlers and fur traders set the stage for glaring misconceptions by Indigenous Peoples of what drinking was all about. Others stress that poverty, trauma and exclusion are the problem, not booze. And still others assert that alcoholism is a learned behaviour, a culturally acceptable norm that results in escape from life that is and has been brutal—ever since explorers and settlers with alcohol arrived in North America.

Many scholarly studies debunk the myth of a genetic connection, including one compiled and researched by John W. Frank, Roland S. Moore, and Genevieve M. Ames, "Historical and Cultural Roots of Drinking Problems among American Indians," which cites the Alkali Lake recovery as a significant example of the positive results of reinstating cultural practices and beliefs, and another by Craig MacAndrew and Robert B. Edgerton, *Drunken Comportment: A Social Explanation.* In the broadcast "Aboriginal People and Alcohol: Not a Genetic Predisposition," aired by the Canadian Broadcasting Corporation on May 30, 2014, Dr. Joel Kettner, associate professor at the University of Manitoba's Faculty of Medicine, states that "there is no scientific evidence that supports a genetic predisposition for alcohol intolerance in the Aboriginal population."

An article by Maia Szalavitz published on the Verge website attests to the link between trauma, low socio-economic status and unemployment exacerbating substance abuse, and states that the earlier the trauma, the higher the risk. The same piece cites Joseph Gone, associate professor of psychology at the University of Michigan, as saying there is "no evidence that Native Americans are more biologically susceptible to substance use disorders than any other group.... [They] don't metabolize or react to alcohol differently than whites do, and they don't have higher prevalence of any known risk genes."

Such works speak of the causes similarly affecting Indigenous Peoples in Canada and the United States. First Peoples in North America took up drinking alcohol because they were damaged en masse by childhood abuse, imposed social structures and the prejudice enshrined in colonialism.

* * *

During the years of change, resolution and revolution at Alkali Lake, rewarding times gradually arrived for those involved in transforming the community from dysfunction and despair to productivity and enjoyment. The First Nation developed a community garden, a logging company, a sawmill and an irrigation system. Most of the populace was engaged in the affirmative metamorphoses that finally enveloped the reserve.

"Special times began to happen and people started to enjoy themselves," Andy says. "Things like getting back to the land, taking up agriculture, getting together with friends, telling stories and fixing houses. There were sober men and women involved with all the groups who kept others from reaching for alcohol, kept them from partying. When I'd attend get-togethers, we'd talk about what we were planning next, what the community could look like in ten years. That was really rewarding.

"Sitting around with some of the guys and hearing them talk about the time they wasted in bars and at parties, all the times they could have been with their parents listening to stories, learning about their culture, and that it was too late—those discussions made all our efforts worthwhile, to know that they recognized what they had missed and that alcohol took all that from them. Unfortunately, some of that still goes on today. There are those who aren't listening, aren't hearing the message others are giving, don't know the truth that drinking robs them of their history, their dignity and a meaningful life."

During the time Andy served as Chief at Alkali Lake, the First Nation's funds increased exponentially, from $21,858 in 1972–74 to $221,446 in 1976 and to $1,429,105 by 1984–85. He steadfastly negotiated forestry agreements with government and area resource companies and applied for provincial and federal grants, among other revenue-producing initiatives. Things were definitely looking up for his people.

Andy would, in the years following 1985, extend his experience beyond the reserve, serving as a director on many boards, such as the National Native Alcohol and Drug Abuse Program, the Williams Lake hospital and a British Columbia ranching and agriculture organization. In addition to her trustee work for the region's school district, in the 1990s Phyllis sat on British Columbia's First Peoples' Cultural Council board for several years, promoting Indigenous culture and language.

Alkali Lake was well on its way to being renewed. The reserve had been ready to get better, to heal. Within fourteen years, it went from 100 percent alcoholic to 95 percent sober.

SHARING THEIR EXPERIENCE
AND BEING BOLD

THE CHELSEAS' FORAY INTO HELPING THEIR VILLAGE FAMILY TO recover and to salvage their lives would prove to be an organic thing. It would continue to grow, to develop offshoots that would ultimately stretch beyond their community. But in the early 1970s, their focus was local.

With the Chelseas' wholehearted support, band members who wanted to get important information to reserve residents started a newspaper called *Alkali Speaks*. It spoke directly to its readers and would operate for five or six years.

Chief Andy was involved with broad village issues, such as "beating the bushes" to produce funding and improvements that would make for better living conditions on the reserve—and he was good at it. As he always did, he spoke the brutal truth, whether it was to forestry companies, environmentalists, ranchers, the school board or businesses, often with the message that the "take, take, take" from their historic lands did nothing for the reserve and had to stop. Andy was also able to work with other Chiefs to get support for what needed to happen. Incremental changes were made, but to this day, the First Nation has not gained its share of nature's wealth in its area.

Simultaneously, Phyllis was dealing with the day-to-day social work duties at the reserve—and she was good at that. "If you want to teach something, you have to live it and have confidence in it," she says. "If I hadn't believed in my own healing and my story, if I didn't believe that things could change, if I hadn't talked about it, nothing positive would have happened. My disclosure encouraged others to overcome their reluctance to speak about personal matters. I had to show them that it wasn't weak to do this, that it could be strengthening.

"When there were issues between a couple, I'd go to their house and bring them back to my small office where we'd talk. I'd tell them that I'd see them again in an hour and that things could not stay the same, that they'd have to make a decision or there would be consequences to their drinking. And I'd suggest that the treatment centre in Williams Lake was a good option. Generally, they'd undergo treatment."

Phyllis's theory was that getting people to communicate positively, rather than from hate and fear, produced healthy results. Her words to them would be "I'm here and I love you. You're family." It was then that they would begin to listen.

The Chelseas would be instrumental in bringing a Lifespring program to Williams Lake. Attendees at its meetings learned how to interact in a supportive and constructive way, very different from what residential school taught them. School meant just trying to survive, and when students left, they had no definitive life skills. Lifespring taught them about loving others. While involved with the course, Phyllis realized that she wanted to become a trainer, that she wanted to do that kind of work—and in time, she would.

But the US-based Lifespring was missing First Nations cultural content. Hence, the group involved with it formed Inner Dimensions and then Core, which brought Indigenous perspectives to the program. From these would evolve New Directions, the Chelseas' organization, which in due course incorporated Indigenous customs, beliefs and spirituality in teaching people a different way to live after sobriety. New Directions dealt with prejudice, racism, restoring self-esteem and respect for oneself and others. The program, still functioning in 2017, grew to include Men's Circles and Women's Circles, both of which comprise much personal sharing, discussion of life changes and mutual support.

From its origins as a home-based business, New Directions would become internationally recognized, respected and in demand. While it was initially set up as a society, administrative difficulties eventually resulted in the organization successfully operating under individual contracts for services, managed by Phyllis, Andy and sometimes, their daughter Ivy. Their reputation and skills would take them to England, Norway, Japan and Australia, throughout the United States, including Hawaii, and across Canada. And wherever they travelled, the same problems existed for Indigenous Peoples. Wherever colonization occurred, societal ills followed. "Struggles and difficulties for Indigenous populations came about whenever someone else moved in and took over," says Andy. "Native belief systems soon would no longer be valid, their way of life would be degraded and steps would be taken to wipe it all out. All the same garbage."

New Directions has expanded to include courses such as Elders Training, Cultural Awareness, Sharing the Alkali Experience, Men's Healing, Women's Healing and Youth Training. Healing the Hurts is a popular workshop that deals with the transgenerational impact of the physical, emotional, mental and spiritual trauma of residential school. The organization's Five-Day Personal Growth Training for ages nineteen and up assists participants to form positive attitudes towards all aspects of their lives through intensive experiential exercises and development.

* * *

The mid-1980s would also bring some noteworthy challenges and meaningful opportunities for the Chelseas, not the least of which was a documentary video of the story of the Alkali Lake Nation's renewal.

Producer and director Phil Lucas of Seattle, Washington, had heard of the Alkali Lake story and approached the First Nation about making a film on it, with the support of Health and Welfare Canada. After much discussion within the community, it was agreed that the documentary should be made. Soon a script was developed, actors were chosen (some, such as Andy and Phyllis, playing themselves), a crew was on site and filming began. *The Honor of All: The Story of Alkali Lake* would prove to be an especially effective tool on a couple of fronts: to deliver the news elsewhere that enormous change can happen, lives can be rebuilt and communities saved, and as an adjunct to the Chelseas' personal messages during their New Directions presentations. *The Honor of All* has been viewed around the globe, and the

Chelseas say the response has always been positive, energizing and empowering for those who have seen it.

"We felt the film could help people," says Andy. "I didn't think it would go where it went or be too big a deal. Thought it might fade after a while, but it didn't. It became a key part of the sobriety movement."

Phyllis adds, "I wasn't sure about having a video made at first and really didn't want to be in it, but got outvoted. In the end, it was a good thing."

She goes on, "From the beginning, it's been the story of the people of Alkali Lake. I just happened to be part of it, happened to sober up before any of the others. I had no plan to make too much of it and I still don't."

Another significant event during that time was a very special 1985 gathering held on the Alkali Lake reserve. The community planned the event, entitled Sharing Innovations that Work, for a few hundred people. In the end, it became a three-day international conference attended by over 1,500.

"Band members presented various workshops; others took care of the organization of all that was needed to serve the attendees," says Phyllis. "And we had speakers on different topics as well as breakout sessions. Four Worlds International Institute assisted with counselling and some workshops, as did sobriety leaders from all over the globe. Andy and I were involved too, but it was a total community effort." Some attendees stayed in nearby Williams Lake. Others camped out on the reserve. Food was brought in, and the sharing that happened went beyond the meals.

The Chelseas feel that one of the best parts of the event was that it revealed to the people of Alkali Lake the many varied resources available to them. It expanded their awareness of the world beyond the reserve and beyond the province of British Columbia. As well, participants had come to meet the community members because *they* were seen as the heroes of Alkali Lake. The ensuing reciprocal communication was positive for all concerned.

Alcoholics Anonymous Powwows[1] would subsequently be held every summer at the purpose-built arbour, constructed in 1985 and located not far from the reserve and the eventual Chelsea property. Their New Year's AA Powwows are also special events. Both these are well attended by local, national and international participants, proof that collaboration works at many levels.

* * *

In 1987, Phyllis and Andy embarked on an adventurous, somewhat risky but definitely courageous undertaking. The reserve no longer suited what they wanted out of life, so they decided to build a new home on land off-reserve.

Well, not *quite* off-reserve—because, in addition to expanding their horizons, Chief Andy wanted to make a very specific point with the federal Department of Indian Affairs (DIA).

---

1   In the past, Powwows were held to mark a successful hunt or victory and included dancing, singing, drumming and food. Today's Powwows are artistic celebrations of being Indigenous and are evidence of the irrefutable link between First Nations peoples and their cultural heritage.

"There was simply no room on the rez for what we wanted," he says. "Our parents and Phyllis and I grew up with horses. We wanted to have horses, corrals and an arena. The family needed a place where we could do the things we wanted to do. We needed space.

"My dad's former father-in-law from his first marriage had negotiated with the DIA for some land in the 1930s or '40s. Dad and I knew about it and liked it—the area, the water, the trees, the wildlife migration trail that crossed it—and that's the spot I chose.

"I knew every boundary of that region, where the reserve started and where it ended; it had been marked from the beginning. Our new house was built with a few rooms on rez land and the rest of it on so called Crown land—my land! Even the corrals and the tack room were also outside rez property."

Several months later, a local rancher who'd been watering his cattle at a pond on the Chelseas' property[2] complained to the DIA about Andy's new fences. A DIA representative soon arrived with questions.

"He asked what I was doing there," Andy says. "I told him I was living on *my land* and that he could get off it! But the fellow replied that the house wasn't on reserve land. I agreed and told him he was on private property. I then asked him if he was speaking for the Queen, and when his reply was no, I told him that finished our conversation. He left. End of issue."

---

2   Phyllis and Andy report that to this day there are issues with ranchers over water rights near their property and adjacent to reserves.

"I was home the day that happened," Phyllis says with a smile. "Andy knew exactly what he was doing. He knew the boundaries and the geography. And he intended to make the government prove that the land actually belonged to the government. We got a mortgage and paid it off in fifteen years. Even had to buy the hydro poles to string electricity to the place, but we did it. Put in a well and heated with wood and propane. Still do to this day."

Phyllis recalls that she had to learn to like living ten kilometres from her friends and all that was familiar on the reserve. With time, though, she grew to feel connected to the surrounding land, loved the space, the freedom it provided. And as she watched Andy build fencing and make improvements, she knew it was the right place to be. It was home.

* * *

In light of this significant step by the Chelseas decades before, it was interesting to learn that, in 2017, Secwepemc activists from the Neskonlith band were erecting compact homes along the proposed route of a pipeline expansion in British Columbia's Interior—building on *their* land, unceded land. The Tiny House Warriors' plan consisted of constructing homes in strategic locations along the 518 kilometres of Secwepemc land the pipeline was to cross. The solar-powered and insulated structures were to be used for language and cultural camps and as shelter for community members struggling to find housing.

No treaties have been signed between government and the Secwepemc people, and although three First Nations had come to agreements with the developer, comprehensive consent was not achieved for the pipeline development project, and resistance ensued.

The United Nations Declaration on the Rights of Indigenous Peoples states that "control by indigenous peoples over developments affecting them and their lands, territories and resources will enable them to maintain and strengthen their institutions, cultures and traditions, and to promote their development in accordance with their aspirations and needs."[3] The Chelseas couldn't agree more.

---

3   UN General Assembly, Resolution 61/295.

STORIES FROM

ESK'ET FRIENDS

DOROTHY JOHNSON, ORIGINALLY FROM DOG CREEK AND THEN Alkali Lake, is a lifelong friend of Phyllis's. Her family also had a Chelsea connection: Dorothy's biological grandfather was a brother of Pat Chelsea, Andy's dad. Phyllis and Dorothy first met at residential school, where their friendship was cemented by the maltreatment they were experiencing. "We both attended Prince George Catholic High School together," says Dorothy. "It was bad there too." But their relationship was good, and was one of the things that sustained them.

After training as a practical nurse in Vancouver during the early 1960s, Dorothy was the school nurse at the Lower Post residential school near the Yukon-BC border and assisted at the nearby reserve as well. On returning to Alkali Lake, she provided volunteer medical services to the Esk'et reserve and was eventually hired. "It was a full-time job," she says, "with part-time pay, but it was needed and so I did it. Even provided first aid at rodeos—I'd be in the stands and the announcer would ask, 'Is Dorothy Johnson here?' I'd wonder who gave them my name. Eventually, I worked under Phyllis at the rez when she was the band's social worker."

When asked about patients' health issues, Dorothy affirms that the causes were related to trauma and conditions on the reserve. "I think the loss of children, the grieving, was a reason too," she adds. "Parents and grandparents crying when they had to leave their kids at residential school and returning to a home with no children there. Having to live without their kids for such a long time. The drinking would start."

Dorothy feels that a family death could lead to alcohol abuse too. "When kids would return to the rez in the summer and find out that a close relative had passed away and they didn't know about it, didn't have a chance to say goodbye or see them in their last days, that was hard."

For Dorothy herself, drinking took hold during an abusive marriage. "I had broken bones and have scars from those years," she says. "But I had to stay, and I drank so I wouldn't feel the pain. Although I was drinking regularly, I talked with Phyllis about it when she and Andy had sobered up. She was someone I trusted. And soon there were seven of us who had given up drinking around the mid-1970s. I went to see Brother Ed Lynch with Alcoholics Anonymous in town, and was the first from our reserve to go to the Poundmaker Native treatment centre in Alberta. Was there for a month.

"When I returned to the rez, my husband and uncle were drinking at the house, so I put a few clothes together and Phyllis picked me up to take me to their place. I was ready to be done with alcohol and that was it. In 1975–76, Shirley Robbins, Evelyn Ignatius and I were the first ones to go to the Nechi centre in Vancouver. Phyllis and Andy had learned about the Nechi Institute: Centre of Indigenous Learning and recommended it. My time there was very helpful. Counsellors encouraged us to learn by doing—and we did. I began to understand things about myself and got some coping strategies.

"There were lots of others who went into treatment after me. But I'd often have kids staying with me once I was sober because there was no food, no wood, no care at home. Their parents were still drinking. One of the girls still calls me Mom," she adds with a smile. "I raised my young sister, Lori, and my brother, Roger, too."

Dorothy reports that the AA meetings Phyllis and Andy arranged were very important as a support mechanism. "But one of their most difficult challenges was trying to keep everyone sober," she says. "And they had to watch out for themselves. Many people on the rez were angry about the changes in the beginning. And it was hard on me too, as the social worker at that time, but I had to stay above everything that was happening. I'm forty-three years sober now.

"Things gradually got better. People were more positive. The rez seemed to be a lighter place. Phyllis and Andy became involved with training and personal growth with New Directions, and I would help with that too. I will always be thankful for them."

She adds, "I didn't retire from the health centre until I was seventy-two. And Phyllis still calls me sometimes when someone is sick."

Her people trust Dorothy. She is one of theirs, knows them, knows their culture and has medical training. Like Phyllis,

Dorothy Johnson is someone they can turn to, someone they can rely on.

Former Chief **Irvine Johnson** is one of the Esk'et First Nation's Yucwenintem coordinators, responsible for Esk'etemc lands, fencing, development and trespass issues. He is also compiling some of the First Nation's history.

"I was born and raised at the Alkali Lake reserve but also attended the St. Joseph's Mission School the same time as Andy, although he was a little older than me," Irvine says. "My early childhood was idyllic, much of it spent with my grandparents up in the meadows. A wonderful time. But when alcohol arrived, we had less and less time with our families because the drinking weekends became longer and longer, often Fridays to Mondays

"At that point, I went out on my own, started working at age fifteen at a ranch in the area and even did some painting during the summer at the mission school. It was good for me to get away, to escape from the horrible times at the rez. It was hell on earth, all drinking and fighting.

"Andy and I were neighbours and friends since we were quite young. I worked at Linde's Sawmill with him and lived next door to him and his family there. When we moved to the reserve, my house was next door to his."

When asked about the beginning of his drinking, Irvine says, "Well, I wasn't a holier-than-thou type. I did drink, just not as much as others."

"During the 1960s," he says, "the band decided to move away from Hereditary Chiefs, and I was the first elected Chief, although my uncle was of the Hereditary Chief line. At the same time, I was also working at a regional school for Native people and eventually talked to Andy about running for Chief, and he was subsequently elected.

"One of the things that stood out for me about what Andy and Phyllis did was their effort to end the squalor that people lived in when alcohol seemed to be ruling everything. The housing program that they and others started, to make repairs and renovations when people were away at treatment, was so important. They'd come back to houses that were fully functional, taps fixed, windows repaired. It made people realize that if they wanted to live in better conditions, they had to do something about it. There were a lot of people tired of the mess that their lives had become.

"The other important thing was that people were getting employment, starting to work, making some money and bringing in an income. So much better than welfare handouts.

"And the Chelseas never gave up," he goes on. "They had to remain consistent, and they did. They stayed sober, no 'on and off the wagon.' They showed that they were really intent on it all. Even if others criticized them for trying to 'better themselves,' they stayed with it. They were being true to the bitter world they saw.

"That trying to pull them down and back into the drinking world was tough for Andy and Phyllis. Even some of their family thought they were trying to be better than everyone else. It was complicated and difficult."

But Irvine saw changes happening, he says. "A brightness was noticeable around the rez. Kids were cleaner, clothes were cleaner. Parents were making changes in good ways. And I think at some point, the 'slowpokes' realized that those who changed were on to something and that was where they could and should be.

"Another important thing that happened was more time was being devoted to kids' hockey and other sports. That was really good. And with the passing of time, it was logical that we were no longer known as the people from 'Alcohol' Lake. The fact that there are kids who grew up never seeing their parents drunk has given those kids a different outlook. They are more positive and willing to accept change as a result of the new norm.

"Still, there are some young people on the rez experimenting, but with drugs instead of alcohol, having their experience with it, but that seems to happen everywhere. Hopefully they'll pull their lives together.

"I think we're still evolving, getting better. It doesn't matter where we are in this journey as long as we're on it together. Some of us have learned of a future ahead of us, that we can go into it with some expectations of better, but that it's all in front of us. How we do it, how we reach it, accept it and handle it is up to each of us."

Phyllis's older first cousin, **Julianna Johnson**, is also a born-and-raised Esk'et First Nation member and was forced to attend the same residential school as her younger cousin.

"When I was sent to residential school at seven years of age, I cried for a week," she says. "I'd always slept with my parents and wasn't used to sleeping by myself on a cot with just one blanket. I was so lonely. Once when I wet the bed at school, they rubbed my nose in it and made me wash the sheet myself.

"Being shipped away to school and how kids were treated there was the root of the band's troubles. Even though my parents were drinking at home, it was still very hard to have no parents around at all."

Julianna recalls that before the community started on its road to recovery, housing was bad, living conditions without electricity were very tough, alcohol was everywhere and fighting and violence were common, with families splitting up and children being taken away by social services. Some of the children never returned.

"One of the biggest things the Chelseas did was convincing people to enter treatment centres," she says. "Going away from their families was hard but for their own good. When I was getting sober, my friends called me names and insulted me. I eventually could no longer talk with them—in some ways, too, I thought I was 'somebody' when I gave up drinking. The AA meetings Andy and Phyllis arranged helped me stay strong, and I learned how to stand up for myself without hurting anyone.

"Phyllis and Andy brought in different help and counsellors to the rez, and Lifespring and New Directions were a big part of recovery. Within a few years, there were more sober people, and I was able to reconnect with friends. It took a lot of hard work and a lot of years, but eventually the band was 95 percent sober.

"The rez eventually had its own school, housing was better and extended family looked after the children of those away for treatment. Keeping kids together was important. Attitudes changed. Parents and kids played together, and moms were walking their babies and toddlers in the outdoors. Sharing happened and good family life developed."

Julianna asserts that her people developed pride and were happy about the improvements that happened. "One of the best things to this day is our yearly AA Roundup. That's a big one for us. It's a great event. Hundreds of people come from all over. Even though my feet aren't good, I help with it—there are seated chores that need doing," she says, grinning.

"For myself, I'm way happier without alcohol. So glad that I don't drink. I doubt I'd be alive today the way I was going. It was a decision I made on my own. And I became proud of my culture and traditions. I have fasted and learned my spirit animal is the bear. I saw it in the clouds, and I'm sure there was one near me, in the bushes. A big bear."

Julianna adds, "I'll be celebrating forty-two years sober soon."

David Ross, a retired social worker, met the Chelseas through his work and their mutual interest in improving people's lives. After working in the Vancouver area, Dave served as executive director of the Fish Lake Cultural Education Centre in Cariboo country in the mid-1970s, during which time he met Phyllis and Andy, as well as Alan Haig-Brown, who was an Aboriginal liaison with School District No. 27. Dave hired (the late) John Rathjen to be in charge of the cultural centre and language development programs.

And so, at a crucial time of adjustment and inclusivity, five people with similar goals and the energy to achieve them crossed paths—and, because of this auspicious happenstance, they were able to bring about significant change.

The Fish Lake centre comprised an eight-room school, a residential dorm, a cookhouse, a recreational area, living quarters for cooks, cabins for students and staff housing. Its curriculum included trades skills, educational upgrading, cultural programming and social services training.

When funding dried up for the Fish Lake operation, those involved with it and others, such as the Chelseas, Freddie Johnson and Charlene Belleau, were discussing the possibility of developing a treatment and wellness centre. This would be the inception of the present-day Nenqayni Wellness Centre near Williams Lake.

Through numerous ups and downs—including starting off in the buildings of the disreputable St Joseph's Mission School— the Nenqayni Wellness Centre would ultimately acquire its own newly built facility on the Deep Creek reserve.

"Initially, we brought in Nechi Institute trainers from Alberta," says Dave. These specialists were able to provide the educational tools and resources to help teach others how to heal the pain and devastation caused by addictions and abuse.

"This played a critical role," he goes on. "We ran a couple of training sessions with the Nechi instructors, and forty to fifty Chiefs, councillors and band members went through that training, which was an impetus for getting a handle on the alcohol problems."

Today the Nenqayni centre includes a full-size gymnasium, a daycare and a family program school, and offers an Elders' Program, continuing care, cultural activities, drug and alcohol information, family alcohol and drug workshops and a Youth and Family Inhalant Program—all of which is summed up in its mission statement: "to provide holistic healing to First Nations and Inuit youth, families, and communities in a safe and secure environment."

Dave also worked with an alcohol and drug program at the area's Friendship Centre in the 1970s and '80s. This centre was a key component of the recovery at Alkali Lake. And so he was again connected to the Chelseas and the Esk'et sobriety movement.

"Andy and Phyllis put a lot of time and effort into wellness programming," Dave says, "and had considerable influence on getting it going. The Alkali Lake story was out there, and having the Chelseas on the centre's board of directors kept things moving forward.

"And at a band level, they were quite ruthless in making social change quite fast. Doesn't happen like that in most communities. It takes a special kind of person to pull that off—to convince people that if they want a better house, they have to be sober. If they want a particular job, they have to show up sober. The Chelseas' underlying message was that people had to make an investment in healing themselves. And they spoke and worked from the heart. What we saw was a much healthier attitude as individuals sobered up. Social activities were dry events, and that had a huge impact, seeing several hundred people having fun without a drop of liquor anywhere. Community development at its best."

Dave thinks the ongoing AA program at the reserve was especially helpful. "The first year was the longest and hardest though. At first it was just Ed Lynch meeting with Phyllis and Andy. But it made sense, and it helped them. Ed was enlightened too. He was a recovering alcoholic himself. Soon others would join the group.

"When I arrived in their area, you never saw a drum, never saw anyone singing or dancing. The only time the church would allow that would be at the end of a funeral. Then the Natives could play their drums for a while and sing their songs. Culture had been stripped. They've reclaimed it."

When asked about Alkali Lake and the Esk'etemc today, Dave confirms that things continue to get better. "So many have continued with schooling and are working on different projects," he says. "We look at Alkali Lake as a leading community in the area."

He adds, "There were exceptional people who came along at the right time. And it's history now."

THE ESK'ET FIRST
NATION TODAY

ALTHOUGH SOBRIETY RESOLVE HAS SLIPPED SOMEWHAT IN recent years, the Chelseas estimate that 60–70 percent of Esk'et First Nation members have maintained abstinence.

Phyllis and Andy suggest that some of the community's youth may be drinking to "get back" at their parents who were involved with alcohol at one time and neglected the family. Others may be entangled with substance abuse because they're bored. An isolated reserve offers few opportunities. Prospects for advanced education and gainful employment are minimal. And leaving their home, their families, their native land and their culture to seek such things presents an immense challenge, both financially and emotionally.

"In today's world, teenagers are drawn many ways and some of them aren't the best," Phyllis says. "If they want to belong, they're going to try to be part of what's available. And for some of them, that won't be a good thing. But how we work with them, how we stay with it, helps us reach out to our youth. It's up to adults to connect with them at some level."

"It's so frustrating and sad to see young people just sitting around, not working, some of them doing drugs and alcohol," adds Andy, "and then complaining that they're going in the hole. Well, of course that's happening; they're not working. They have no income. And there doesn't appear to be the initiative to create work. The reserve's sawmill is sitting idle. And the few people who have jobs with the band are just hoping they can keep them. There are more non-Natives working for the band than Natives.

"And it's not just a training issue. Racism still exists. I think it's getting worse. There's more prejudice against developing an economic base for us than in the past. Years ago, we all worked in the same mills with white people. It was a friendly environment. Nowadays, there's little of that. My sons have difficulty finding work."

"Companies hire non-Natives before First Nations," says Phyllis. "Native people have grown by leaps and bounds in many areas of our lives, but white society doesn't see that. And we deal with racism every time we go to town."

"Indigenous people simply want a share of the region's economic development," Andy asserts. "Lumber is piled sky high at Williams Lake; the sawmill runs twenty-four hours a day with three shifts. It's all Indian timber, but how many Indian people work there?

"One of the biggest problems for Alkali Lake is that we're not near a large city. We're out of the way, thirty miles [fifty kilometres] from Williams Lake that has a population of ten or eleven thousand. First Nations bands closer to large cities can rent out property to non-Natives at sky-high rents because they want to holiday there or live there. That can't happen here. Economic opportunities are very limited."

Some of the bias against First Nations people as employees undoubtedly stems from the endemic difficulties faced by those who came out of residential schools in the past—so damaged, so troubled they could barely function—and returned to a village trying to drown its pain.

It is well known that education and health services for Indigenous communities were insufficiently funded from the outset. And the results are clearly evident in the truncated schooling, the personal harm, the societal malaise and the abnormally high death rates among Indigenous Peoples in Canada. It's been no different at Alkali Lake.

With the 2015 publication of the Truth and Reconciliation Commission of Canada's final report, the change in the federal governing party and a ruling by the Canadian Human Rights Tribunal in 2016, this unfair situation is being addressed. Additional funds have been allocated for health, education and reserve policing, along with the restructuring of Indigenous and Northern Affairs Canada, which has been divided into two departments: Crown-Indigenous Relations and Northern Affairs Canada, and Indigenous Services Canada.

One of the stumbling blocks to effective provision of health and education benefits to First Nations is that they are funded federally but delivered provincially. This has led to confusion as to responsibility, along with drawn-out legal battles over who is accountable for what.[1] And caught in the middle of such

---

1   Lavallee, "Honouring Jordan."

machinations are those who urgently need the issues resolved and the essentials provided.

Phyllis and Andy report that community meetings are no longer well attended on their reserve, unless members are directed to be there. If small amounts of bonus money are attached to attendance, the turnout is good. Otherwise, very few take part. "There's not the sense of community these days, not like there once was," Phyllis says. "There's no exchange of ideas with council, no consultation at band meetings. Just information given out. I think people feel powerless—it's tough to stay on the reserve, but there are no answers in moving to a city or town."

As on many reserves, fetal alcohol syndrome is prevalent at Alkali Lake, Phyllis says. "It's a big issue. We're aware of it, but it's difficult to remedy when there isn't enough funding for psychological intervention or programs on the rez to help with it. Money is needed for more medical staff and additional resources."

As described by the Chelseas, there are few, if any, doctors who rotate through reserves as visiting physicians. The remote locations of many Indigenous communities make this difficult, as do Canadian winter weather conditions. So when an Indigenous patient does manage to get to a doctor, the physician may know little about that patient, who then feels like a "number," just another case.

The Chelseas point out that education will be the obvious key element in providing trained First Nations professionals to practise in reserve clinics. Promotion of healthy living, along with support in that effort, is paramount for sustained recovery.

Phyllis believes that the food her people are consuming has been a problem. From the near starvation and malnourishment at residential school through to today's store-bought items, their health has been compromised by what they eat. "Our diet once consisted of game, fish, vegetables and berries," she says. "Today's overprocessed products contain many preservatives, lots of sugar and fewer nutrients, in my opinion. It's very different from the past, and I don't think it's been good for us. Add to all this tight finances and restricted access to better foodstuffs, and you've got people eating cheap fast food, junk food and soft drinks.

"Our rez maintained a large community garden in the 1980s and '90s. But there was more money available for tools and supplies then. It takes cash and effort to establish and maintain a grow-your-own food supply. Now there are just a few private gardens on the reserve. It's easier just to head to the store."

Then there's the "white syndrome"—Phyllis recalls that her homemade jams and preserves were considered "too Indian" by the young people around her, who wanted to be like those outside their community.

Yet early Indigenous Peoples had been very active—sourcing their food took strength and persistence, as did making shelter and clothing. Led by wildlife migration paths, salmon runs, berry crops and the seasons, theirs was a traditional nomadic lifestyle involving much hard work. In addition, they faced a "feast or famine" situation: food, though healthier then, was sometimes scarce, and therefore energy storage was a priority for survival.

When colonizers arrived, however, their demand for bison, beaver and fish drastically reduced the natural food supply.

Soon Indigenous Peoples were deprived of their land and life-style. Shunting bands onto small reserves with few natural resources and expecting them to adopt agriculture as a way of life was literally another death sentence for their customs and eventually for so many of their people.

Present-day access to inexpensive but less nutritious foods can lead to energy being stored as fat, increasing the risk of obesity-related disease.[2] Adding to this recipe for ill health, today's reserve life is sedentary compared with the past, Phyllis confirms. Vehicles—rather than travelling by foot or horse-back—are the primary mode of transport, if a family is lucky enough to be able to afford a vehicle and fuel. Employment is hard to find. Television and computers can lead to a lot of sit-ting. Despondency and depression may limit what an individual is capable of doing. Poverty and lack of access to a nutritious and ethnically appropriate diet are factors. The changes from their usual foods of the past, from their vigorous lifestyle and to their sense of self have been nothing but negative for Indigenous Peoples and have made them susceptible to being overweight and developing disease. "This has happened world-wide," Phyllis says.

Numerous medical studies and reports have revealed alarm-ing rates of type 2 diabetes mellitus and its related amputations, coronary heart disease and kidney disorders among Indigenous people. The epidemic-like Canadian statistics are frightening: up to 40 percent of adult Indigenous people develop type 2 dia-betes, compared with 7 percent of the general population, and

---

2   "Our History, Our Health," First Nations Health Authority, http://www.fnha.ca/wellness/our-history-our-health.

they are diagnosed ten to twenty years younger as well. Their diagnoses peak at age forty to forty-nine versus over seventy in the overall populace. Incidence of diabetes is three to five times higher than in other Canadians and has doubled in the last ten years in many areas of the country.

Indigenous women are particularly susceptible to gestational diabetes, which can be a predictor of post-pregnancy type 2 diabetes and can also lead to an increased risk of diabetes in their children. This begs the questions: How closely is the condition of a pregnant woman followed, given the limited health services available on reserves? What monitoring is carried out? And what treatment is prescribed to ward off such a condition?

Sadly, the Chelseas know only too well the consequences of a diagnosis of diabetes and insufficient medical help. "Our son Dean died due to diabetic complications as a teenager," Phyllis says with a catch in her throat. "We had very little information about the disease years ago and lost Dean because of that. Our youngest, Owen, also has diabetes but manages it well because we were able to obtain a lot of guidance about dealing with the disease early on."

* * *

As Andy and Phyllis assert, Indigenous leaders and peoples must decide what they can do, what they require and what needs to be in place to improve their health.

Answers will be found within their communities and will come from Indigenous citizens. Only those living within restrictions can determine what will free them from the bonds.

Governments, organizations and citizens must truly listen, must get beyond the guilt of being descendants of those who perpetrated the wrongs and injustice, drop defensive shields. And take action.

Despite the variable needs of the 634 First Nations, the Métis and the many Inuit communities of the North, we can hope that a consensus on general reparations will be reached that will benefit the majority. It will take ingenuity and it will take compromise—and it will take money. Had the inherent problems of colonialism been addressed years ago, the cost would probably be less. But that didn't happen. And so Canada must now pay for its negligence.

Then there's the judicial system and how it deals with First Nations people. For Indigenous and non-Indigenous offenders alike, it falls terribly short. As Rev. Dr. Peter Baldwin, a former corrections chaplain who has seen the worst side of prisons, says, "Jails often simply produce better criminals." There are certainly psychopaths who should be incarcerated for life, but in the case of many offences, prison is not the answer. A jail sentence or banishment from a reserve simply avoids dealing with the origin of the problem. Restorative justice and rehabilitation have proven to be effective and to produce long-term positive results.

"Putting someone on probation or parole creates a lot of additional problems for that person, someone who probably has little money and has no car to get to their appointments, with the probation or parole officer fifty kilometres away," Phyllis says. "The one obligated to report perhaps needs medication or to eat regularly if they're diabetic. Can't something better be developed that takes all this into account? Years ago as a court worker, I told judges this and asked for changes. The justice system is still a mess!"

In 1999, the Supreme Court of Canada sanctioned Gladue rights for Indigenous offenders[3] under which reports are to be prepared defining how the accused had been affected historically by colonization, oppression and intergenerational dysfunction. Yet across Canada, Gladue entitlement is being ignored, underfunded or denied. Add to this the fact that there are so few writers trained to compile such reports and you have a step in the right direction that has gone completely off course.

Land claims have become a lucrative industry for litigators. As Andy says, "Resolution cannot be achieved unless we, the principals to the issue, are negotiating face to face, sitting at a table. Yes, get some legal advice, but have the lawyers sit way in the back somewhere."

"I agree," Phyllis adds. "Government officials sitting down with Elders and Chiefs, nation to nation. It's complex and will depend on the level of growth that's happened for and with Natives. We're different everywhere—one meeting might have a few attending and another may have one hundred. Attention is on the rise and we're speaking up. APTN [Aboriginal Peoples Television Network] is informing large numbers of our people.

"Everyone, on both sides of the situation, needs to be willing to meet, to listen and to talk meaningfully. And I don't think today's Native young people are going to put up with the nonsense that's been doled out in the past."

"Governments and corporations need to share," says Andy. "They don't share. So why should we give them anything?

---

3   Edwards, "Canadian Injustice."

Forgiveness or anything else? They just take and then expect to be treated with kindness. That's baloney. In fact, it's bull-shit! Native peoples have survived by sharing everything—game, tools, land, work. How about co-operating with us, just live with us? If our lives have to change, others have to change also. The next Native generation may not be so kind.

"If we're going to survive together as Canada, First Nations have to be looked at as human beings, not property. Corporations need our agreement for development. Aboriginal knowledge and scientific knowledge can work together. We'll both be right."

Phyllis feels the same way and hopes the next generation will get more involved. "Young people need to take part in the decision making, start speaking up. Some older band members are stuck in the past, in mission ways, doing the same things, not challenging Indian Affairs and a society that oppresses our communities.

"The shame of who our ancestors were, of who we are, and the indignity of poverty that was imprinted on us in the past is still with us today. Impoverishment and hardship were forced on us. With help, we can overcome all of this. It's a good thing that others outside our people are becoming aware of what's happened. But knowing about it and doing something about it are two really different things. It will take a lot of effort and joint co-operation.

"Band councils and staff in some places are entrenched in old methods, following the rules, strictly by the book. They need to take a stand for their people. Forget about being in control and focus on what is best for their community, even if it means shaking things up. As I said, maybe it will be young people who will bring about change in the near future."

LEGACY

IT IS SAID THAT A TRUE TEST OF WORTH IS FOUND IN AN ENTITY'S longevity and its replication, whether that be the worth of a system, of an attitude or of people. To this could be added recognition by one's peers. In light of this, it is apparent that Phyllis and Andy, with the support of family and friends, have ably shown that resolve and strength can effect monumental change. They were and are examples of the triumph of the human spirit over almost insurmountable challenges. The fact that others have followed their lead in retrieving communities from dark nadirs speaks to the point that those outside their circle believed in their methods. Although never ones for personal bravado, the Chelseas have been acknowledged as leaders and as a couple who cared from the depths of their being, who reached out, who grasped the hands of those needing help—and who, as a team, were unafraid to demand better from those in authority, to speak their truth, to discuss the tough stuff and to live their beliefs.

The year 2017 marked the Chelseas' forty-fifth sobriety birthday. Such an accomplishment says it all. It illustrates unshakable conviction and the ability to adhere to a decision that defied habit and mores in 1972. The respect they engendered was not looked for, but it was without doubt earned.

Phyllis received the Order of British Columbia and was awarded an honorary doctor of laws from the University of British Columbia (1991) recognizing her teaching and her efforts on behalf of others. With the realization that professional and culturally appropriate help was needed to deal with First Nations' alcohol problems, Andy connected with health centres to implement this. In addition to the Nenqayni Wellness Centre in Williams Lake, Maple Ridge Treatment Centre in Vancouver, Round Lake at Armstrong, and Poundmaker's Lodge in Edmonton, he was involved with numerous treatment clinics throughout British Columbia, often serving on their boards of directors. Andy was feted and presented with a splendid headdress by thirteen First Nations Chiefs in Alberta recognizing his contributions to the sobriety movement. As well, the City of Williams Lake bestowed municipal recognition honouring Andy's initiatives.

The ongoing invitations to speak at conferences and to present workshops through the years conferred respect for the couple that went far beyond their immediate community.

When asked what they hope their stories, as told in this book, will accomplish, Andy and Phyllis both see beyond the personal, envisioned possibilities and speak of others.

"I think the book will be a new tool to educate people," Andy says. "How far it will go I don't know, but some will read it all and learn from it. And it will push for change."

Phyllis adds, "I hope the book will bring about hope itself, that there is hope in having what we need in life to be happy, to stay connected to who we are as Native people. I expect it will encourage people too. It's important we realize that, as First Nations, we have strength, and that we have a responsibility to pass this on to younger generations. We must tell them that hope and strength have always been with us, and have been passed down through families. We must carry it in our hearts and send it forward."

A LONG GOODBYE AND
A SWEET HELLO

IN JANUARY 2017, ANDY, HIS FAMILY AND HIS FRIENDS RECEIVED sad and serious news. He had been diagnosed with untreatable cancer. The big bear of a man was under attack by something he wasn't going to beat. But what he could do, he did. Andy carried on, changed his diet, began taking First Nations medicine, kept working and interacting with others and continued to smile.

In his indomitable way, Andy also persevered with the extensive interviewing necessary for this book. The storytelling and opinions were discussed at length an hour at a time. Throughout those bittersweet conversations by telephone over hundreds of kilometres, there was the sense he was gradually slipping away.

It was difficult not being able to see Andy and Phyllis in person, as a result of the distance and the winter weather that prevailed in 2017. But as spring arrived in British Columbia's Interior, I planned an overnight trip to the Cariboo-Chilcotin region where they lived. Although rather fatigued and with a new sadness in his eyes, Andy looked reasonably well, and he, Phyllis and I enjoyed our time together.

The second day included a road trip up the Fraser River valley to places significant to Andy and to his people. Now taken over as ranchland, a flat plateau that had been the sacred burial ground of his ancestors awaited the desecration of spring planting by the current rancher. Farther along the gravel road, far across the broad expanse of river valley, sat the remnants of his granny's cabin, where he'd been born. And as far as the eye could see, the earthly origins of the Secwepemc people stretched before us—the land they had traversed on foot and on horseback, where they had hunted and gathered, drummed and sang, where since time immemorial they had lived and died.

As I listened to Andy, watched him take it all in, the bond between Indigenous Peoples and nature was readily apparent. That relationship was intrinsic to him, passed on to him in the mountains by his grandmother, nurtured by his family and taught by his First Nation's Elders. And try though they did, those running St. Joseph's Mission School were never able to destroy all that existed within him.

The trip to Andy and Phyllis's homeland and residence was informative in many ways, not the least of which was that what had been taken from them was much more than simply property—the core of their being had been stifled. A lifeline had been severed, and those who perpetrated that severance were utterly blind to what they had done.

As spring became summer, it was approaching six months since Andy's diagnosis, and he'd been with us much longer than had been expected, longer than many might have survived. And although it wasn't discussed, the end was approaching. It would come June 27.

Andy's memorial service was poignant and attended by hundreds. His family had lost a much-loved husband, father and grandfather. His community had lost a leader. And First Nations had lost a resolute flag-bearer, someone who spoke his mind—a man who swept away the detritus of government meddling and corporate excuses. Qluwenk, whose foresight blew away the clutter of colonization and laid bare what was critical to his people, a Chief who stood atop a mountain of two centuries of suppression and declared it had to stop.

Many lives are greyer with his passing.

The summer of 2017, remembered as "BC Burning" in some circles because of the devastating wildfires that engulfed the province, would also prove to be trying in other ways for the Chelsea family. While still grieving, Phyllis, her daughter, Ivy, and her granddaughter Carmen and her husband, William, would be evacuated to Kamloops, driving the back roads through fiery timber and dense smoke, for Carmen was expecting her first child within days and medical services were being shut down in Williams Lake.

While living in a Kamloops hotel and eating in restaurants, but close to a hospital, the family would welcome a beautiful baby girl, a granddaughter, Andy and Phyllis's great-granddaughter, on July 21—coincidentally the day in May celebrated as Andy's birthday each year.

A joyous event amidst their collective sorrow. And the baby would be named "Andi."

MEMORIES FROM THE
NEXT GENERATION

THE CHELSEA CHILDREN

IT CAN BE SAID THAT IVY, DEAN AND ROBERT, IN THEIR CHILD-hood years, had quite different parents than did Kevin and Owen. Although they had good hearts, young Phyllis and Andy, at their core, were troubled. The daunting hangover from residential school would haunt them for decades, and would bring hangovers of a different kind even as they attempted to raise their family with love. Drinking regularly overtook them as teenagers and young adults—alive, but battered and bruised emotionally, psychologically and physically.

Alcohol, anger, arguments and the physical abuse of Phyllis sporadically permeated the lives of the three eldest Chelsea children, with implications for them at various levels, although, as previously written, Dean would succumb to diabetic complications as a teenager. The Chelsea parents' recovery in their late twenties meant that younger siblings Kevin and Owen, as well as the older three, would benefit from the love and wisdom of Andy and Phyllis without the black shadows that had intermittently enveloped an otherwise affectionate and caring home life.

IVY

Ivy Chelsea is an amalgam, a fusion—just as iron and carbon become steel, combined elements resulting in a stronger substance, she is that. With the strength of her father and the innate kindness of her mother, Ivy is able to walk multiple paths with assuredness. Even as a child she demonstrated these traits and was instrumental in helping her parents forge a new life.

Although the Chelseas' early marriage included tough times, there were many good times too. "One of the best was riding horses," Ivy says, smiling. "Yep, we rode horses every day, Dean, Robert and I. Even arranged our school schedule to allow for riding lessons Dad organized. And then there was hockey. Dad played a lot of hockey, just like his dad. And he started a boys' hockey program at Alkali. When I saw that the boys played all the time, I whined about it enough to him that we got a girls' team going, the Pink Panthers. I still have my jacket from that team.

"Another thing we enjoyed were the driving trips, piling into the truck with our parents and being shown different places, special places for Mom and Dad. We'd drive to Mom's meadow where she grew up, and Dad's too, and stay in the old cabins there. Ride horses, put up hay, go swimming. A great time for kids."

However, Ivy's early childhood was also one of contrasts: the fun times with her parents and the dismal times witnessing their trauma-induced dysfunction, when her dad was drinking and angry, and her mom was drinking and the target of his anger. When Andy and Phyllis were off on a weekend of partying, she would stay with one of her grandmothers, whichever one would not be imbibing that weekend. These times with her Kyé7e (grandmother) confirmed to Ivy that non-drinking times were right times. She began to understand the connection between alcohol and violence. And so, at age seven, when her mother arrived to pick her up at the end of a partying weekend, Ivy refused to return to the family residence.

"I wanted things to be better at home," she says. "I told Mom I wanted to stay with my Kyé7e and that I wouldn't let her take Dean and Robert home either, that I would help Kyé7e look after the boys. Mom told me that if we came home for good, she'd never drink again. That was more than forty-five years ago. She kept her promise."

About difficult familial and personal times, Ivy says, "I got to know what I didn't want and they made me stronger. When I was a teenage mother and getting involved with drinking, the diabetic illness and eventual death of my brother Dean was a turning point. Troubled over his hospitalization and learning that he was never coming home, I turned up at the hospital drunk. Mom and Dad were so upset that I'd been drinking that neither of them would go into Dean's room with me. I went in alone to my unconscious brother, and when I returned to the waiting room, Mom had words for me. She told me that I'd been her and Dad's biggest support when they quit drinking and that they needed me now. And she asked if I really wanted to start with my own baby what I had hated about their drinking. Did I want to start that with my own child? My answer was 'No.' And then she told me to go get a coffee and think hard about my answer and what I was doing. That was the beginning of the new me."

When asked what the toughest thing about living on the reserve was, Ivy replies emphatically, "The gang rapes."

"I fought off two rapes and I witnessed them happening to others," she says. "When I was twelve years of age, I was chased but fought off the one who caught up with me—it was a relative! I trusted him. Other girls had set me up and then left, told the boys I was alone at the school, and they waited for me.

"There was some counselling back then, in the seventies, but not many went. And the incest and assaults go on to this day. Abuse often leads to abuse, from generation to generation. It needs some serious attention."

Ivy recalls that she was a young adult when her mother and father built their house and moved off the reserve. "It was good for them, the move. It gave them a sense of place and space, a sense of control. And it provided a break from dealing with the troubles on the reserve."

Ivy would eventually be mother to five children: Carmen, Amanda, Keith, Kiki7 and Cucle7, and would ultimately raise them on her own following the end of a disastrous and hurtful marriage. "But," she says, "I consider myself lucky, because I had the support of my parents. Lots of women do not have the help I had. It was a challenge, but I was able to survive it, and my kids are strong, all living off-reserve."

At the urging of her mother, who was an educator, Ivy pursued teaching as a means of supporting her family. As well, in her early twenties, she began assisting her parents with their training sessions, bringing, in due course, the message of sobriety and healing to thousands over the last three decades.

"There's a lot that's rewarding about the training and workshops," Ivy says, "but the long-term friendships made during them are very special. It was through such a friend that I was convinced to tell my parents about what I'd endured in my marriage. It was the hardest two hours of my life, but in the end, it was healthy. Dad kept giving me tissues with his hand on my shoulder and Mom held me. I knew after that there was nothing that I couldn't tell them, and they knew there was nothing they couldn't tell me. My life has been an open book since."

Ivy remains inspired by, and somewhat in awe of, her parents' accomplishments. "Mom operates from the heart and Dad operated from the spirit. Mom has a gentle energy that calms people, and just Dad's presence was strength. Others knew not to mess with him, not to try to con him. My parents could get to the heart and spirit of someone's problems. They knew very well the impact of the worlds of Indigenous people, whether in North America or elsewhere. If I had to describe them in one word, for Mom it would be 'love,' and for Dad, 'compassion.'"

ROBERT

The fondest early memories of the Chelseas' second son centre on times when the family was up meadow. "Dad would let me be adventurous, going out into the bush," Robert says. "Then there was hunting, fishing and horseback riding. I loved being around horses and breaking horses. Dad taught me well because it was a bit dangerous too. Eventually I'd go with Dad and his team to rodeos. I'd round up the cattle, open gates, settle them down. I played hockey too, on a team Dad coached."

Robert would eventually be certified as a Red Seal carpenter, having demonstrated the knowledge required for the national standard in that trade. "I trained at the Nicola Valley Institute of Technology and returned to work at the reserve," he says.

"I like that carpentry lets you see something come together and gives you a good feeling when it's completed. Wood becomes something special. There's creativity to working with it."

When asked about his relationship with his parents, Robert reports that in the 1970s he would have liked to have had more time with his mom, whom he describes as very caring. "She and Dad were doing some good things working with others, but sometimes I missed them both. And Dad was awesome, but you knew there were things you didn't do around him. There'd be a definite signal. I think he liked that I was a bit of a rebel and adventurous and that I got pretty good at sports."

Actually, Robert was more than "good" at sports—he excelled and could have gone a long way in hockey, according to Phyllis.

"Mom and Dad almost cared too much. They weren't into the sobriety movement for the money. They were and are good people. Never let greed take over, just took care of others. I'm proud of them."

He adds, "They worked very well together. Mom had strength besides caring, and you definitely knew when she was serious about something. Dad was a good backup for her and she for him. They were thorough. My mom is involved and engaged—and she isn't shy—and Dad was seriously caring and funny. There were lines you didn't cross with him, and lines he didn't cross. He'd always speak his mind.

"My parents always encouraged me to be proud to be Native."

KEVIN

Kevin Chelsea describes himself as cocky, supportive, a former logger, a teetotaller, a quick learner when it comes to computer software and as having the entire world at his fingertips through the internet. To that could be added storyteller, given his colourful reminiscences of working with his dad.

"My entire life it felt as though Dad treated me as an equal," says Kevin. "When I was a young kid, we were out hauling hay bales and he needed a driver. Dad told me to jump in the driver's seat, showed me the stop and go pedals and told me to go slow and try not to run over the bales. I proceeded to run over more than one bale, but we got the job done and I learned how to drive.

"When I was older, we were clearing a road to the meadow through a rarely used back road. Dad couldn't run the chainsaw, drive the truck *and* move the trees. So according to Dad logic, it was only natural that I run the chainsaw. He handed it to me and said, 'This is the switch for on and off. This is the pull cord. Yank it. There it goes; now cut that tree. I'll move it. Any tree across the road, cut it.' So that's how I learned to run a chainsaw. A couple of years later, Dad started a logging company, and next thing I knew, I was standing on the landing, measuring and cutting giant logs.

"Once we were walking back to a landing, chainsaws over our shoulders, and Dad stops and looks up at this one tree. He then looks down the skid trail[1] and says, 'I bet you ten bucks I

---

1   A temporary, non-structural pathway over forest soil created
      by dragging or "skidding" felled trees or logs from a stump to
      a log deck.

can hit that stump over there from here with this tree.' Well, I'm a cocky bugger so I take him up on it. The tree is leaning way over and I doubted he could do it. Silly me—Dad had been felling trees for decades. I'm watching and it looks like he's going to miss, but he swings it at the last second and he hit the stump! Sometime later, on payday, I'm in line to cash my cheque, and as soon as I have the money in my hand, I feel a tap on my arm. I turn around and there's Dad with a big grin on his face, hand out, waiting for his ten bucks."

Through it all, Kevin reports that while he and his dad remained father and son, they also became friends. "Dad never talked down to me, never dumbed down anything, and he taught by example," he says. "I learned that leaders lead from Dad."

One of the most difficult things Kevin observed on the Alkali Lake reserve was the gradual return to alcoholism by some community members. "Because I believed in what my folks were doing back then, I lost a lot of friendships with people who were drinking," he says. "I asked my dad once about why he didn't just ban alcohol when he was Chief. He said, 'Because alcoholism is a disease.' I guess it would have been tough to tell those who were drinking, 'Although we know this is how you deal with all the crap of residential schools and a tough childhood, and even though many things have already been taken away from you, now we're going to take alcohol too.'

"And I grew up seeing too many people go before their time. Life can be slippery out here. You see people fall and get up, but some just can't get traction again and you don't know how to help."

Kevin would eventually become an information technology specialist with A+ certification in computer repair, and he works in that field today as part of his job.

"I didn't really decide to get into computers and IT," he says. "It just happened that I was good at it. One of my strengths is that I learn how to use software fairly quickly, and learned website building, not as technical as website development, but it's useful. Technology keeps changing and we can only try to keep up."

Speaking of family life, Kevin says he thinks he has had a different relationship with his parents than anyone else in the family. "With Mom, she can come to me and let me know exactly what's going on, and I listen with an understanding ear. When there are decisions to be made concerning family, I just let her know what I think and how I feel about something, you know, give her my insight and experience—tools, giving her tools.

"Our parents were harder on us than anybody else. I mean, they didn't go nuclear, with yelling and such, but a look of disappointment from them was far more effective than anything else. They made sure we were cared for, fed and had a safe place to call home. Trust was a big thing, and I never broke that trust. My parents taught me that my mistakes would be mine, no excuses, no blaming someone else. And that's what Snewt [Owen] and I try to provide to our family today."

With regard to the achievements of Phyllis and Andy, Kevin describes how his parents set the examples that helped the Esk'et community choose sobriety. "They got the band running in a better direction with policy and hard work," he says. "It was a massive undertaking for a couple surrounded by people who were sick, dying and/or dangerous. I'm nervous when I have to deal with one person who's angry. Mom and Dad dealt with a whole community. That's a kind of bravery I admire and can only try to emulate. They made me try harder for my community.

"Dad was the sensible voice and Mom was the constant motivation. I mean, they still are, even though Dad is gone. Every day I can hear him in my head telling me that I should do this or that—but sometimes I have to trust in myself. Mom tells me when my ideas are good and that I need to get on with them. What we really miss is that Dad was a filter between the family factions—well, I'm joking, but he did keep us from arguing sometimes. He kept us compartmentalized and Mom kept the lines of communication open—still does. Now that Dad isn't here, now that we just have his wisdom, we're all trying to fill a giant pair of shoes."

Asked for one word to describe his mother, Kevin immediately says "caring." And for his father, his word is "strength."

OWEN (SNEWT)

The youngest Chelsea offspring, Owen, also called Snewt, had to be brave as a child; perhaps having inherited much of his parents' strength, he learned, at a young age, to effectively deal with type 1 diabetes and all it involved.

He and brother Kevin also managed to get along without much time with their sought-after parents, who were in high demand as leaders in sobriety initiatives nationally and internationally. "It was just the way it was then," says Owen. "We stayed with Mom's mother, Kyé7e Lily, when Mom and Dad were travelling. Sometimes at Kyé7e Anastasia's but mostly with Kyé7e Lily."

Growing up on the reserve, Owen and his friends learned to fear the RCMP. "We knew that someone was in trouble or something bad was happening when we saw the RCMP on the rez. If they took someone away, that person was bad."

About dealing with diabetes, he says, "I had to watch everything I ate and inject insulin but I needed social outlets too—I was glad that I had a motorcycle to travel around and connect with my friends. I may have missed out on some things like birthday parties and camping trips because I felt that I couldn't go due to the health problem.

"And Dad was always teaching us stuff, kept us busy. Things like repairing vehicles, ranch work, feeding cattle, fixing fences. He'd show us once and then we had to figure it out for ourselves until we got it right. We still depend on that learning and determination today."

Owen has considerable artistic ability, something that was encouraged by several art teachers in Williams Lake. His professional training and work, however, took him in a different direction: geographic information system (GIS) mapping.

"The main reason I wanted to learn about GIS," he says, "was because I realized that for First Nations to be recognized in treaty negotiations, we would need maps that could prove where we were from and who we are."

When asked about his parents' successful undertakings, Owen replies with a smile, "My mom has an honorary doctorate of laws and is also a recipient of the Order of British Columbia. I'm very proud of her. And Dad accomplished so much in his life. I was so pleased for him when he was invited by Alberta First Nations Chiefs and was presented with an honorary headdress in Edmonton, now a treasured keepsake within our family."

He adds, "Mom and Dad made decisions together. But Mom would carry them through, with Dad always there to support her. He would, of course, often make decisions on his own—he was a very smart man—but mostly they operated as a team. They came up with great ideas together."

Owen says emphatically, "My mom is always honest, and Dad was and is wise."

We should be grateful for nature's generosity, something I've learned from Indigenous peoples. They acknowledge the source of their well-being, clean air, clean water, clean food and clean energy—all things that are created, cleansed or replenished by the web of life around us.

—Dr. David Suzuki

AFTERWORD

RESEARCHING THIS BOOK HAS TAUGHT ME MUCH—THE PAST and the stories of First Peoples in Canada, the widespread impact of colonization, and that one's origins can lead to a very different life within our borders.

The outlook for Indigenous Nations in Canada is inevitably coloured by the past, and the historical picture painted is not a pretty one. The incongruously named Doctrine of Discovery legitimized rights to lands "discovered" and arbitrarily judged *terra nullius*, that is, land owned by no one, empty of (Christian) inhabitants, prior to European declaration of authority. This overreaching doctrine resulted from the papal bulls *Dum Diversas* (1452), *Romanus Pontifex* (1455) and *Inter Caetera* (1493), which were issued by Roman Catholic popes to Spanish and Portuguese monarchs in order to spread Christianity to non-European peoples. British and French royals soon adopted this application of power for their own exploratory ends—and thus justified their rule over Canadian territory that they considered *terra nullius*.

In June 2014, the Supreme Court of Canada unanimously decreed that "the doctrine of *terra nullius* (that no one owned the land prior to European assertion of sovereignty) never applied in Canada, as confirmed by the *Royal Proclamation* of 1763."[1] Also of note is that the United Church of Canada has completely renounced the Doctrine of Discovery, which, it states, "led to the subjugation of all conquered peoples in every imaginable way." In 2012, its General Council Executive approved a motion that the United Church join the World Council of Churches in denouncing the Doctrine of Discovery.[2]

In a document dated March 19, 2016, entitled *The "Doctrine of Discovery" and* Terra Nullius: *A Catholic Response*, the Canadian Conference of Catholic Bishops (CCCB) stated the following: "We believe that now is an appropriate time to issue a public statement in response to the errors and falsehoods perpetuated, often by Christians, during and following the so-called Age of Discovery. In light of all this, as Catholics:

"1. We firmly assert that Indigenous people, created in the image and likeness of God our Creator, ought to have had their fundamental human rights recognized and respected in the past, and that any failure to recognize and respect their humanity and fundamental human rights past or present is to be rejected and resisted in the strongest possible way;

---

1   Tsilhqot'in Nation v. British Columbia, 2014 SCC 44, [2014] 2 S.C.R. 256.

2   *Repudiation of the Doctrine of Discovery*, United Church of Canada, 2017.

"2. We firmly assert that there is no basis in the Church's Scriptures, tradition, or theology, for the European seizure of land already inhabited by Indigenous Peoples;

"3. We reject the assertion that the principle of the first taker or discoverer, often described today by the terms Doctrine of Discovery and *terra nullius*, could be applied to lands already inhabited by Indigenous Peoples;

"4. We reject the assertion that the mere absence of European agricultural practices, technologies, or other aspects common to European culture could justify the claiming of land as if it had no owner;

"5. We reject the assertion that Europeans could determine whether land was used or occupied by Indigenous people without consulting those people."

In May 2016, under the banner "The Long March to Rome," a delegation of Indigenous leaders was granted a brief face-to-face meeting with Pope Francis and were able to make an in-depth presentation to Cardinal Silvano Tomasi of the Pontifical Council for Justice and Peace, requesting that the Doctrine of Discovery be rescinded. The council agreed to review the issue and to consider abolishing the ancient papal bulls.

* * *

Due to what has happened—and also what has *not* happened—over the last two centuries, the prospects for Indigenous populations appear complex. The shortcomings within the labyrinth of rules and regulations that control and limit Indigenous Peoples' lives are abysmal and, in any other segment of our society, would be entirely unacceptable. The ninety-four

Calls to Action contained in the final report of the Truth and Reconciliation Commission glaringly confirm this.

Given the morass of past legislation, the current structure of government departments and the widely varied needs of First Nations, Métis and Inuit communities, restitution and righting of past wrongs undoubtedly will take time, money and joint co-operation. Regardless of such tough parameters, a fair and equitable future for millions of First Peoples in this country depends on action and implementation.

It is encouraging that, in 2017, the Canadian federal Liberal government supported a parliamentary bill in process that demands full implementation of the comprehensive United Nations Declaration on the Rights of Indigenous Peoples, which establishes a universal framework of minimum standards for survival, dignity and well-being of Indigenous Peoples of the world and elaborates on existing human rights and fundamental freedoms as they apply to specific situations of Indigenous Peoples.

A grassroots movement, aptly named Circles for Reconciliation, was started in Winnipeg in 2016 by Raymond Currie in consultation with First Nations Elders and groups. Its purpose is to facilitate meaningful dialogue between Indigenous and non-Indigenous individuals. Small gatherings of eight to ten people, including at least three Indigenous persons, meet weekly or biweekly, ten times. Sitting in a circle and using a talking stick or eagle feather, participants each have the opportunity to speak, to ask questions or to give answers, under the guiding principles of dignity and kindness for all. Interest in this initiative has grown, and get-togethers are being held across the country.

KAIROS Canada, an ecumenical organization working towards action for human rights and ecological justice, has developed an interactive learning experience called the Blanket Exercise, which teaches Indigenous entitlement history. This innovative workshop definitively reveals five hundred restrictive years of Indigenous past in one and a half hours. Facilitators lead participants through the experiences of Indigenous Peoples in a way that engages them emotionally and intellectually. A debriefing session allows for discussion and feedback, often in the form of a talking circle.

In 2017, a $6.8 million federal grant funded the C3 (Coast to Coast to Coast) Expedition that eventually brought together four hundred Canadians—Inuit and non-Indigenous—over the fifteen legs of its 150-day voyage on the *Polar Prince* from Toronto to the northeast coast of Baffin Island en route to Victoria. The on-board discussions around reconciliation, among other issues, were oftentimes difficult, acrimonious and awkward—as were the silences.[3] The exchanges during the sea journey revealed that there is much work to be done—but at least it is starting.

In early 2018 Canada's federal government set up $20 million in funding to support survivors of sexual violence, including Indigenous, immigrant and LGBTQ2 populations, as well as seniors, disabled women and those in remote communities—part of a strategy to confront gender-based violence through research, prevention and support groups for victims.

***

---

3   Ian Brown, "Confronting Race, Shame and Reconciliation."

The topic of violence must include an extremely troubling situation unearthed while this book was being researched—the alleged rape and assault of Indigenous women in police custody, specifically in the custody of the Royal Canadian Mounted Police.

The relationship between Indigenous Peoples and the police has long been troubled, beginning in the nineteenth century with the government-mandated North West Mounted Police involvement in the forcible removal of Indigenous children to be placed in residential schools, a role assumed in 1920 by the RCMP. And it has, in some locations, deteriorated badly since then. This is not to say that all officers are tainted; a positive first-hand account described how two incidents of harassment of a female Indigenous RCMP constable were dealt with effectively by the sergeant in charge at a detachment and stopped immediately. However, stories do exist of officers who are racist, sexist, misogynist or bullies.

These accounts describe an insidious condition that has developed for First Nations women, especially within small and remote communities. It is known that threatening her children will quiet an Indigenous woman, that she can be violated and then continue to live with ongoing fear, and that she risks being unfairly judged, punished and sentenced by someone who is charged with protecting her.

While it is of course nearly impossible to report an assault when the perpetrator is part of the local police force, it is also increasingly difficult for Indigenous women to obtain medical attention and provide DNA evidence, as hospital staff are obligated to call in the RCMP. The police will ask for identification of the offender, and if the victim won't give a name, she may be suspected of lying or prostitution.

Numerous news reports and studies to be found online tell of alleged strip searches of women by male officers, physical battering, threats of deadly harm and sexual assault. Prosecution of officers can take years, and very few cases result in convictions.[4]

Police forces are necessarily imbued with power and control as part of keeping citizens safe by enforcing the laws of our country. And they are respected for their role in this, as well as being trusted to perform justly and to the highest criteria. Betrayal of this authority and trust, even by a minority of officers, is unacceptable, reduces our democratic rights to shambles and threatens what the majority of Canadians value—a just civilization.

A report by the New York-based non-governmental organization Human Rights Watch (HRW), released in 2013, reads like a horror story of alleged RCMP abuse among British Columbia's Indigenous women in rural communities, describing rape, pepper spraying and tasering, police dog attacks and physical abuse of women and girls, among other offences.[5] The group's 2012 investigation was carried out over five weeks in ten northern BC towns and involved eighty-seven interviews with fifty Indigenous women or girls aged fifteen to sixty. The lead researcher, Meghan Rhoad, stated that approximately a dozen

---

4   "Complaints and Allegations Against Police," Ontario Human Rights Commission; Leamon, "Canada Has Its Own Demons"; Palmater, "Police Violence in Ontario."

5   Canadian Press, "Mounties Raped, Abused BC Aboriginal Girls"; Grant, "Report Submitted to Ottawa Highlights Police Abuse"; "RCMP Accused of Rape," CBC News.

young women cancelled their interviews because they feared retaliation from police working in their small communities.

Media Relations at the RCMP National Communication Services in Ottawa provided the force's statement, dated February 2017, in response to the HRW report on police misconduct in northern BC and the subsequent investigation by the Civilian Review and Complaints Commission for the RCMP (CRCC).[6] The CRCC probe investigated body/strip searches, policing of public intoxication, interaction with youth, use of force, domestic violence and missing persons issues. The commission reportedly found no systemic misconduct by RCMP members in northern British Columbia, but did identify weaknesses or gaps in policy and procedure that resulted in thirty-one recommendations for improvement, all of which were implemented by May 2017.

Human Rights Watch also conducted six weeks of fact finding in 2016 during which sixty-four Indigenous women and social service providers were interviewed in Saskatchewan at Prince Albert, Regina, Saskatoon and rural communities in the north and central regions of the province.[7] Degrading strip searches, groping by male officers, physical assault during arrest, fears of police harassment, threats, intimidation and racial discrimination were part of the final HRW report, according to the Canada director for HRW, Farida Deif. She also stated that a key issue was that there hadn't been much progress on

6   "RCMP Response to Chairperson-Initiated Complaint," Royal Canadian Mounted Police.

7   *Submission to the Government of Canada on Police Abuse of Indigenous Women*, Human Rights Watch.

accountability, without which there is no deterrent to future police abuse.

An RCMP statement addressing this Saskatchewan report, issued on June 19, 2017, outlined expanded actions taken as an adjunct to the CRCC changes reportedly put in place by May 2017, namely regarding Indigenous training, de-escalation and crisis intervention training, respectful response, missing persons investigations, female body searches, violence in relationships, identification of dominant aggressor, and race and gender data collection.[8]

Heart-wrenching stories of abuse ostensibly at the hands of police, told with changed names or anonymously because of fear of retribution, are part of the fabric of Canada. Dedicated, honourable police officers and the masses of good men within our country must persist with women to call out those who prey upon women, to insist on justice and to demand consequences for crimes committed—no matter who commits them.

* * *

Yet another bleak facet of injustice against Indigenous Peoples warrants attention: institutionalized discrimination. A recent CBC Radio town hall forum of *The Current* held in Vancouver addressed, in depth, the issues facing Indigenous patients within hospitals.[9] Diane Lingren, provincial chair for the Aboriginal leadership caucus of the BC Nurses' Union, and Tania Dick,

---

8   "RCMP Statement on Human Rights Watch Report," Royal Canadian Mounted Police.

9   "Indigenous Nurses Call Out Systemic Racism," CBC Radio.

member of Dzawada'enuxw First Nation and president of the Association of Registered Nurses of British Columbia, described incidents that hark back to the worst of the "bad old days."

Diane Lingren spoke of how an intoxicated non-Indigenous person entering an emergency room is fed, calmed down and sent by taxi to a shelter—in sharp contrast to her report of seeing RCMP called in when an Indigenous patient arrived inebriated, who then handcuffed that patient's ankles to their wrists and took them away in a police car.

Tania Dick described her family's "Sinclair story"—a stark reminder of Brian Sinclair, a forty-five-year-old Indigenous man who was found dead in his wheelchair in 2008, thirty-six hours after his arrival at a Winnipeg health centre ER, never having been treated. An aunt of Tania's had fallen in her bathroom and hit her head, and as a result was confused and staggering when she arrived at emergency. Physicians diagnosed her as intoxicated. Eighteen hours passed in that emergency department with no higher level of care provided, even though her condition deteriorated, and she died as a result of her injury, Tania said.

The two nursing professionals also described physicians who erroneously believe Indigenous patients have different pain receptors and therefore require lower levels of narcotics to cope with pain.

Diane's reports of lack of care or negligence, although wholly supported by some physicians, have resulted in retribution and veiled threats during closed-door meetings with her superiors.

The joy apparent on the faces of First Nations patients when they see a nurse of their own ethnicity coming to care for them says it all. As Tania stated, "Terrible though it is, they're just excited to see this brown face."

When asked about discrimination as described by the two nurses, the BC Interior Health Authority replied, "Concerns raised about the treatment and experiences of Aboriginal patients and staff are taken very seriously. There are no clinical practices or policies at Interior Health which are based on race or ethnicity.

"Involving the RCMP in situations in emergency departments is a last resort."

It would seem that there are definitely cases in which the theory of practice and policy never makes it to the ER floor. The unequivocal mandate must be: "Do no harm."

* * *

Looking ahead, sharing of Indigenous culture and wisdom and partnering in economic development projects are examples of positive steps towards recovery and reconciliation for Indigenous Peoples, as are self-determination and land title resolution.

The first National Gathering of Elders, held in Edmonton, Alberta, in the fall of 2017, was attended by more than five thousand leaders from Inuit, Métis and First Nations communities. Its purpose was to share and honour the knowledge and insight of Indigenous Elders with a view to helping shape the next generations.

The collective wisdom that emanated from that assembly can only be regarded as a definitive road map for personal and communal recovery. Guideposts such as sharing Indigenous culture beyond Indigenous communities, embracing that culture, being proud of who you are, respecting Elders and enjoying family are crucial to the journey. The compelling statement that twenty-four drums beating together in rhythm are powerful and symbolic medicine must resonate with all who see cohesion among Indigenous communities as crucial to reconciliation.

Instruction in skills such as hunting, fishing, storytelling, sewing, tanning and beading do much to strengthen the time-honoured and long-standing traditions within Indigenous communities. The National Aboriginal Council of Midwives is striving to have an Aboriginal midwife in every Indigenous community. The point was made that birthing in the hands of women themselves, carried out with respect, knowledge and sincerity, is the way Indigenous babies were meant to be born. Retaining language, it was said, is vital to sustaining a people's history, essential to one's sense of self, indeed to the core of a community—one that honours the past as it prepares for the future.

Increasingly, Indigenous communities in Canada are partnering in renewable energy projects and simultaneously producing thousands of jobs. It's reported that nearly one-fifth of the country's power comes from facilities fully or partly owned and run by Indigenous communities, creating 15,300 direct jobs for Indigenous workers and $842 million in income. Although such economic development is not easily available to small communities, establishing natural renewable energy sources on Traditional Territory where possible is seen as another step towards reconciliation and economic development.[10]

---

10   McDiarmid, "Indigenous Communities Embracing
       Clean Energy."

PHOTOS

Andy Chelsea, age fifteen.

Phyllis (Squinahan) Chelsea, age fifteen. Andy and Phyllis became friends as teens. Their friendship would develop into a loving relationship of fifty-three years.

Andy's mom, Anastasia (Charlie) Chelsea.

Phyllis's sister, Lorraine (*left*), with Andy's sister, Vivian.

Vivian in traditional dress.

Phyllis's mother, Lily, holding Ivy Chelsea. In front is young Phillip Johnson.

A young Phyllis, wearing a cowboy hat and leaning against the hood of the car.

Pierro Squinahan (Phyllis's father) and Patrick Chelsea (Andy's father) preparing to compete in "Roman racing" at a rodeo.

St. Joseph's Mission School. The barn and outbuilding are on the left, and the white building with the windows on the right is the school. Courtesy of the Museum of the Cariboo Chilcotin

St. Joseph's Mission boys hockey team, 1955. Hockey was a welcome break from the rigid routine of work and school. Courtesy of the Museum of the Cariboo Chilcotin

A young Andy at his favourite pastime—riding horses.

Dean Chelsea, age about twelve years.

Andy on the right (in the cowboy hat), enjoying a New Year's feast with his family.

Phyllis receiving an honorary doctor of laws degree from the University of British Columbia.

Daughter Ivy, an educator like her mom.

The Chelsea siblings. *Top left*, Kevin; *seated left to right*, Owen, Ivy and Robert.

Appendix I

INDIGENOUS LEADERS
SPEAK OF THE FUTURE

AS A MEANS OF SEEKING INPUT FOR THIS BOOK PROJECT FROM
local First Nations, interviews were conducted with Elders,
Chiefs, councillors and educators on the topics of the present,
the future and hope for Indigenous Peoples within this country.
Excerpts follow.

Frank Antoine currently serves on the Bonaparte First Nation
council. He is the chief executive officer of Moccasin Trails
Tours, director and board chair of the Thompson Okanagan
Tourism Association and a board director for Indigenous
Tourism British Columbia. He also formerly served as First
Nations liaison and marketing representative at Quaaout Lodge
& Spa on Little Shuswap Lake in B.C.'s Southern Interior.

When asked how he manages council duties and his additional obligations, he replies that he's very good at scheduling.
Other things Frank is good at are planning and communication—in addition to seeing the big picture for his First Nation.
His mantra has become *Knucwentwecw*—"working together,"
whether that be interacting as individuals, dealing with the past

in order to form the future, recognizing ethnic origins or walking two paths in different worlds.

"The reason I returned to my band and became a council member was because I'd gone out from it, learned what the world had to offer and then came back after going through a healing process. Not all people can do that or attempt to do that. Some see the rez as a bad place. Yes, it has its bad aspects, but that's where we're likely going to be buried. Some don't return until that time. And that's a big disconnect they create for themselves. Past history can be learned from and growth can come from that. It's important to have a balance of outside world and your band's culture, language and beliefs.

"However, within First Nations communities, trauma has been the number one thing in people's lives and still is in a lot of ways. Some say they don't need to understand it because it wasn't part of their life. But that's been part of our culture and we have to reach back and grab it—wrestle it into submission. The balance can be found in the Medicine Wheel: the physical, mental, intellectual and spiritual. The ones who find that balance find hope and faith that sustains them. Some of our good history was built around plants, animals, water, trees and our relationships to those. We're passing that on to many of the next generation so they will be the stewards of all that.

"We, as Indigenous Peoples, now have the opportunity to grow and learn and be part of society. From my perspective, we need to quit looking at what has happened in the past, stop holding on to it. Acknowledge it but learn to let it go."

Frank reports that when welfare was introduced to his community, it began to fall apart. "We used to help each other. That's not the case now. Everyone wants something from the band in what's become a codependent, enabling relationship. It has become a way of life for some, although there are independent types who want nothing to do with that. But when I go home, mostly what I hear is anger and bitterness, and it isn't just about non-Natives. It's between band members, within the community. Some haven't changed their attitudes for many years. Nor did I. I didn't change until I was in my early forties, when I realized I had to do things differently. Some call it finding the Red Road. Whatever it was, my life turned around."

The Bonaparte First Nation is administered through Elders groups and committees that work on specific components, such as natural resources, highways and culture. A comprehensive community plan sets out where the community wants to go, and a strategic plan describes how to get there.

"We want members to have a voice," says Frank, "but we need them to participate. If a system is going to work effectively, it has to hear from everyone, not just a few people. Chief and council have to encourage all band members to get involved, attend meetings, state their opinions, know they are being heard. Everyone needs to be a part of the vision. Working together is the foundation of a community. There has to be a connection between leadership and the band. As Senator Murray Sinclair, former head of the Truth and Reconciliation Commission, said recently, "Think outside the box but stay in the circle." That's so important. Leaders have to be doing what they do for the right reason—for the people."

He says emphatically, "I speak my mind but I listen too. I encourage band members to come to council, to sit down and talk, to speak up, but many of them don't know how or don't feel comfortable with that. Sometimes it's the drama or politics at the band office or within council that keeps them away. So I go to their home. We visit. We talk. But I tell them that I can't be their puppet, that I can't continually speak for them, that they have a bigger voice than council. They put us on council and they can make us take care of the community in the best way. We need to hear from them, to work together to work things out."

Asked to comment on the Indian Act, Frank replies, "It's complex. And it's an excuse to be used against the government and something for the government to use against us. We're at the point where we're both trying to go downriver in a different way. Sometimes we have to paddle upriver but are we paddling together? No. It's the system and its rules that don't work, not the people.

"Another flawed thing is the justice system. It needs restorative sentencing, and needs to change. Sentences are being shortened because there's no space in the jails. And so many inmates are Indigenous. We need to police ourselves, help each other until the authorities and court procedures catch up. The other part of it is that incarceration has become a lifestyle for some Native people. They see something they can take advantage of, knowing the consequences—so they serve six months, have six months of freedom and then go back to jail. That's their choice, Indigenous or not. They become codependent. I don't judge them for that—I grew up with some of them. I know the difficulties they've had, and they've chosen a path that to them is easy. But it's really a double-sided sword in lots of ways.

"Education, including cultural awareness, is critical to our people and needs to be funded adequately. My classroom is everyday life, and learning for me is ongoing, but I spent time in school and had the chance to graduate. All First Nations young people should have that opportunity. However, it's an individual choice. Change comes from within, through a one-on-one with yourself every morning in the mirror."

Frank adds, "I balance two worlds. Culture isn't just a job to me; it's a lifestyle. Has to be. It has to have a purpose in both the worlds that make up my life. Creating values within myself that allow me to be connected to business and still be connected to the land creates a good base. It's the now and the future I'm concerned about more than my past. I don't hold on to anything from my past that's hurt me, but I recognize that it's helped develop me."

Dean Gladue can trace nearly 350 years of unimpeded Métis bloodlines on both sides of his family, which originated in the Red River area of Manitoba. "I'm the last of the nomadic Métis," he says. "A fifth great-grandfather, Cuthbert Grant Sr., and his son, Cuthbert Grant Jr., are my ancestors."

Cuthbert Grant Jr. (ca. 1793–1854), of Scottish and Cree or Assiniboine descent, was born near the Saskatchewan-Manitoba border and became a Métis leader who guided his people to victory at the unplanned clash of Métis and Selkirk settlers in 1816 known as the Battle of Seven Oaks. He founded Grantown (later St. François Xavier), was appointed warden of the plains by Hudson's Bay Company governor George Simpson and, with his followers, provided for and protected the Red River Colony over at least twenty-five years.

Nonetheless, Dean reports that the Métis were a forgotten people—accepted neither by non-Indigenous settlers nor by First Nations, and unacknowledged by government, outside of forcing some Métis children into residential school. "We were caught between two social orders," he says, "except that Indigenous bands were being oppressed too. Métis, in the past, were able to help First Nations and were instrumental in providing food to them when Indian agents were rationing it. That positive history between our peoples has never been acknowledged or written."

Beyond his significant family history, Dean has led a productive and interesting life, which includes junior hockey and competitive baseball, twenty-six years as a police officer with the Royal Canadian Mounted Police and a recent entrepreneurial initiative that once again connects Métis to First Nations.

"When I was involved with sports and looking at possible occupations, one of my teammates was a Mountie who told me the RCMP was looking for new recruits," Dean says. "Seemed like an interesting career choice, and I was soon writing their initial exam, and the rest, as they say, is history. When I joined the force, some of my family saw me as going against the Métis people—when you look at the troubled history around the Riel Rebellion, you can see why. Growing up I'd been a bit protected from all that negative stuff so I didn't really understand why my family were so disapproving of my signing up. But I believe everything happens for a reason, and I carried on."

Dean was categorized as a "special constable," a past designation that defined Indigenous officers and meant they would never wear the red serge of the force's dress uniform. The special constable program ended within the RCMP in 1991.

"I was in an all-Native troop of thirty-two recruits from across Canada. Part of RCMP training is to tour the RCMP museum, and there we came across a glass case with a rope inside it. We were told that rope hung a traitor—and the traitor was Louis Riel. I'll never forget that moment in my life. With a sick feeling in my gut, I told the corporal that Riel wasn't a traitor, that he was a hero to us! But it didn't stop that tour guide from continuing to say Riel was an enemy and a killer. I almost quit that day."

Another disconcerting situation for Dean happened during rigorous depot training. As new officers, Dean's troop marched behind more senior troops. However, even when he and his all-Indigenous colleagues became a senior troop, they never were moved from the rear. The discrimination was obvious.

"I soon realized just how racist an organization the RCMP was," he says. "I often *felt* the racism rather than experiencing it. But because of my stubbornness, I faced it all head-on. They weren't going to get the best of me.

"And from the beginning, I felt that being on the inside could help bring about change. I always said what needed to be said, which didn't make me the most popular guy on the force. But not speaking up just wasn't an option."

Dean would serve in several First Nations communities over the years, and he eventually heard about residential schools for the first time, which led him to ask his mother whether she'd been sent there. "In a very quiet voice, she answered 'Yes,' and then went on to say she couldn't talk about it. There was too much pain. That made me break down, finally understanding some things—and that the RCMP had been the collectors. It had never been spoken of in our home. I was beginning to realize, to put things together about the oppression our people had endured."

As president of his local Métis community, Two Rivers Métis Society, Dean sees not only the overall situation of his people, but also the incremental parts of improving their lot and eliminating discrimination. Preserving distinct Métis customs and beliefs is essential, as is proof of lineage to Red River Métis origins, which should include Cree or Ojibwe, and French, Scottish, Irish or English ancestry. Funding for better education and training are also important. Dean says that those in authority, whether policing agencies or government, need to develop compassion when it comes to dealing with Indigenous Peoples, that they need to be made accountable for their actions, learn and improve. As well, he recognizes the internal problems that exist within the RCMP and is hopeful that effective action will be taken to end the abhorrent actions of some officers.

"Native and non-Native need to work together to make it better. Everyone wants to live in a safe world, no matter what colour our skin is. It's a pivotal time in Canadian history. We all have to face the evil past, then look ahead and move forward without making the same mistakes. Continue to keep talking. And yes, it's true—the world needs love, more love, with no race or colour attached to it."

He adds, "Indigenous Peoples should stop kicking the ground—that just trips you up. Look to the stars. Believe in yourself. If we're going to heal, we'll have to heal together. Native people are the force that can create that recovery."

Dean firmly believes that knowledge is power, no matter what an individual's interests and gifts are. It could be gained through art, writing, sports, a profession, activism or a trade. Each person's journey is different, as is how they get to their destination.

"My motto is 'Think locally but learn globally,'" he says. "I believe that's especially critical for those living in remote communities. They were, as were we, once nomadic people following the seasons and the food supply. Being confined to one spot is unrealistic for them. Funding and food sources are what's needed. Whenever you have modern living clashing with traditional ways, there'll be challenges. But for isolated communities, teaching kids to find a balance by spending time in the bush, living off the land and getting in touch with their roots goes a long way towards giving them purpose."

Dean continues, "In my experience, one of the biggest issues for First Nations is the internal politics within communities. It amounts to reverse discrimination. Old animosities and jealousies have to be let go of for the good of all. Speaking up is critical to this.

"Some will say that alcohol or substance abuse is the problem. No, it isn't. It's a symptom, a crutch to numb the pain. Giving up alcohol isn't the solution if the individual isn't feeling better about himself or herself. Getting sober has to go hand in hand with getting well inside."

When it comes to the justice system, Dean recognizes that there are some who have to be put behind bars for the safety of others. "The predator, the child abuser, the psychopath—you don't want them out, but maybe if there was intervention earlier in their lives, could they have been saved from themselves? Could their crimes have been prevented? For most of those in jail, treatment centres and treatment plans are needed as part of incarceration. Restoration is needed within a person to change their behaviour. Jail can become a revolving door. Without rehabilitation, jails are just holding facilities."

This former law enforcement officer believes that the right to a Gladue report must be in place for every Indigenous defendant. Dean is probably the relative of the Indigenous woman, Jamie Tanis Gladue, whose 1999 Supreme Court of Canada case led to the development of the report meant to describe an Indigenous defendant's history and background for sentencing consideration. Colonial oppression, generational residential school confinement, poverty and the reserve system absolutely affect the lives and actions of those subjected to such negative conditions. Funding and facilitating these Supreme Court-mandated reports is necessary to fair adjudication and restorative justice for the accused.

"But I'm an optimist," Dean says with a slight grin. "We've come a long way. There's still a lot of work to do, but at least we're willing to change. Some might disagree with me, but I still say progress has been made and I'm proud to live in this country. To make it right, we need to continue talking and listening. The next big thing will be the expulsion of the Indian Act—or the Communist Act, as I call it. It's all about control. This will happen, but are we ready? That will be up to Native populations."

Dean Gladue's most recent undertaking is a resource management company started with partners George Jennings and Zach Parker. TSAA Resource Management has been set up to assist First Nations to control and understand their resources, to manage treaties and to decide what's in their best interests.

Harking back several hundred years, this tripartite enterprise is once again providing a bridge between Métis and First Nations peoples, to help them navigate the road between modernity and tradition—with governments and corporations, between non-Indigenous ways and Indigenous purpose. Having a foot on each path will stand the company in good stead.

Ronnie Jules, besides having dedicated much of his life to his community and to improving the lives of Indigenous Peoples, was Andy Chelsea's "best bullshit buddy," as he was affectionately known.

"I'd known Andy for about forty years," he says with a smile, "and we became close over the last ten years or so."

Like Andy, who was active within the Alkali Lake area and beyond, Ronnie served on the Adams Lake First Nation council for over thirty years, fifteen of those as Chief, as well as with the Union of British Columbia Indian Chiefs, the Secwepemc Cultural Education Society and the BC Elders Society. In addition to post-secondary education, this broad spectrum of interaction, along with his involvement in large economic development projects, has provided Ronnie with a constructive overview of what would be important to the Adams Lake people—as evidenced by the resource income the band receives and reflected in the community's development of its health centre, a spiritual centre, the Chief Atahm Immersion School—the only one of its kind in Western Canada—and the Adams Lake Recreation Conference Centre.

"We built a lot of our community around sports and coaching," says Ronnie. "Hockey and baseball—people love sports here. And annually we spend over $100,000 on it all. But the best education comes from the 'University of Secwepemc'ulecw'— every morning when you walk out your door, you're there, you're in class, you're in a large classroom. You pay attention, learn and listen to your people and to nature around you."

Ronnie recalls that one of the worst days for First Nations was in the summer of 1964, when they were allowed to buy and consume alcohol openly. "It was the saddest day in our history," he says. "For the next fifteen years, we were on our hands and knees, crawling through our lives. On skid row in cities and in ditches on the land. Forty percent of us died right away, and some are still dying today. Trauma and alcohol are a bad combination. But thanks to people like Andy Chelsea and what the band at Alkali Lake did, most of us are on our feet again. The Chelseas led us in the direction of good, down the pathway of a better life again.

"They pushed for treatment centres, worked at setting them up, which helped hundreds of people, but funding for the centres today has been cut back and needs to be restored. The problems haven't all gone away."

Education is a key component of First Nations recovery, according to Ronnie. "It is our tool, and it's happening in a good way," he says. "Our Elders have been saying that for years. And Indigenous foresters, RCMP, nurses, teachers, lawyers and nurse practitioners are all being trained, just to name a few.

"Co-operation, pulling together for the common good, is important, the way it used to be. Things have changed now. Our Chiefs are not appreciated as they once were. People are watching to see if they step out of line. Some of this starts from what happens outside the band, what's shown on television and in provincial elections. It's as though our traditional honour has been lost, and it must be restored again.

"Working with governments, other Shuswap bands and surrounding towns and cities are all part of being in unison with the world around us but maintaining our culture and aiming for self-government. We have strong people in all our communities, but if you're not riding in the same wagon on the same road, it's not going to work. Transparency means everything.

"Years ago declarations by Chiefs were put in place to bring us together, to act for the good of our community and Nation. Band members wanted us to work together then, and they still do. 'Sign and honour your signature' was the message. Working together is critical to moving forward."

Ronnie adds, "We have never ceded our Traditional Territory or title to it. Restitution for what was taken from us is essential to self-determination, to reconciliation and to coming together with governments. Land has always been at the centre of the difficulties."

When asked what, in general, is the major issue for Indigenous Peoples, the former Chief sighs before saying, "I'm a storyteller but it's difficult to put exact words to it. There seems to be a lack of spirituality, of going back to our cultural ways using sacred things, such as the pipe, tobacco, sage, sweetgrass smudging. When people pray around ceremony, they can't lie or be bitter. Other bands use sacred traditions to create the setting for meetings, for discussions. I hope our band will soon be ready for more of that. We have some of the area's best hand drummers, singers and dancers here.

"Former chiefs, like Andy Chelsea and Fred Johnson, did more than can be put into words. Andy was a 'professor' of Shuswap law. Those guys were the best. What they did for their people needs to be honoured.

"There are a lot of answers required that will come from different people, different territories and different situations.

Agreement will probably be difficult. We need to get to know each other from band to band and decide what would be best for all in the big picture, and then work out the details for individual communities."

Tammy Mountain, whose origins are with the Xaxli'p and St'át'imc First Nations, is the district principal of Aboriginal education with British Columbia's Gold Trail School District 74, which includes nineteen communities within three Nations: the St'át'imc, the Secwepemc and the Nlaka'pamux. Having lived both in large municipalities and within a reserve, Tammy is someone who clearly understands the complexities of retaining one's heritage and traditions while functioning in the modern-day world.

"A big part of my role is to bring awareness and understanding to our schools and staff," she says, "and to the students about the history and the impact it's had on our community. I talk about reconciliation and what it means, not just to Indigenous people but to all Canadians. I also provide information about white privilege and the understanding of that. Just being made aware of it brings insight."

Tammy believes education is an important building block to improving lives. "Not only do we need to have educated people running our communities, because it all goes back to 'The more you know, the more you know,' but also when we have people running social services or health programs, there needs to be a certain level of education; otherwise, those programs will not do justice to the community. A lot of the time, community members depend on those agencies, and uneducated staff are no benefit to them.

"We need to educate our own people and our own communities. But it's been that they don't want to leave their communities. It's getting better, and I think opportunities are increasing as well as the realization that education is important."

Besides supporting culture and language in her district's schools, Tammy gives presentations on reconciliation, white privilege and stereotypes. "They are interactive sessions for principals and teachers that result in a lot of conversation and awareness around those topics," she says.

"Knowledge is where we have to start with our students too. They need to clearly understand, because they get a lot of ideas and information from various sources. Working together to provide a foundation for students is critical. I think that's where we're going now in education: people understanding more. We need to start at a place where we're all healing at the same time and moving forward together."

Asked what changes she thinks are needed in the education system, Tammy says, "I think we just need to keep moving ahead, keep building relationships. We've started talking about the impacts of residential schools and the Sixties Scoop, but now we need to dig deeper. It's more than the impact on those who were removed or sent to residential school. It's also about the following generations and how they've been affected.

"Education today, the whole concept of the new curriculum from K to nine, now has Indigenous content embedded throughout all subject areas. It's about land-based learning, and it's a great place to be right now in education. I'm looking forward to what's to come."

Tammy adds that her responsibilities include organizing culture camps with staff, teachers and principals. "We go into

Indigenous communities and learn about their local culture, language and history," she says. "We've been doing these camps for four years now, and they've been very successful. They provide a really good snapshot of Native communities. Our school district is 62 percent Indigenous population. Staff should be aware of who their students are and where they come from."

Former Chief **Roger William** of the Tsilhqot'in Xeni Gwet'in First Nation was elected Chief at age twenty-five and would become part of his people's Indigenous Rights and Title case initiated in 1988 by previous Chiefs and Elders. Their 1989 Nemiah Declaration, written in Tsilhqot'in and English, stated that nothing was to happen on their traditional land or reserve without their involvement and that they opposed clear-cut logging, mining and dams.

"I grew up knowing our leaders were fighting the government over a British Columbia hydro project that involved draining three lakes for a dam that would put the Nemiah Valley under water," he says. "Protecting and preserving the Tsilhqot'in watershed was a stand I took to naturally."

The Tsilhqot'in case, which dragged on for years, would include litigation, negotiation, roadblocks and resource agreements, culminating with an eventual 2014 milestone decision by the Supreme Court of Canada that ruled the Tsilhqot'in and Xeni Gwet'in had proven beyond a doubt their title to 1,750 square kilometres of Tsilhqot'in traditional land. It had been a difficult journey, but amazingly, they had won.

Roger feels the title win will pave the way for other First Nations who are working through land settlements or legal actions. He and Tsilhqot'in leaders hope it will also serve as a positive example, leading to even better outcomes in the future.

"The Tsilhqot'in warriors who fought and died for our land and people like Chief Andy Chelsea were our inspiration," he adds. "Since winning our case, we've been travelling and meeting with other First Nations to exchange ideas and information in the hope of encouraging them to go after reclamation of their rights and lands.

"That's a tough thing to take on, though, because so many of our people are still dealing with the impacts of European settlement, residential school abuse, the smallpox epidemic and ongoing racism. All of that leads to the use of alcohol and drugs. Even some of our leaders and staff are controlled by substances. And those who get into leadership by deceit or manipulation are eventually found out and are not re-elected. Re-election needs to be based on a person's honesty and the balance they bring to the job. We're healing as communities and learning fast. And although there are some young people who are lost, there are some who are incredible, who are strong and who will be in for the long haul."

Roger adds, "We do a lot of circle discussions in our community and at the Nation level. Circle meetings with families and communities are very important.

"For remote First Nations communities, I think being out on the land could be funded, along with education in culture and language. There are a lot of First Nations leaders pushing for more communities to get kids out of the classrooms and out onto the land. The classroom should *be* the land. Investing in our children is so important. Before the Europeans, our children were involved in all activities and work. We need to get back to that. And if internet were available to everyone, they could learn their language, culture, more about nature, math and English through it. Elders and members could help with that.

"And another important part would be teaching survival skills, out in nature, about water, trees and the soil. Our people used to live off the land. Life skills can be learned through that knowledge. If economic development is limited in remote places, teach the next generation how to use the land to survive. That's invaluable."

"Western education is an answer no matter where Indigenous people are located," Roger says. "However, including our trad itions is important too—I feel maybe more important. Getting First Nations professionals on a reserve is a plus. They know our ways, the language, and they have the training to help others.

"The most negative thing, the major issue, for Native peoples was and is the abuse they've suffered. The deaths that were caused, the communities that were wiped out, the reserve system under the Indian Act, the generations of harm that continue to this day, all have to be overcome. Healing has to take place. Changes are needed—must happen—both within and outside our communities.

"Two key parts of all that are resources and recognition. We're pushing for that, to have what we need to be able to govern ourselves in areas of education, health care, social work, housing and creating our own economy. We have a lot of educated people available to do all that, but financial resources are needed as well to maintain jobs that allow community members to stay in their villages rather than go off to the city for work, leaving their culture and history behind. Funding would allow us to catch up as a people in terms of healing, learning, self-government and development of a sustainable economy."

On the topic of consensus among the more than six hundred First Nations bands within Canada, Roger believes it is possible and that the reserve system was bound to founder in areas critical to the well-being of those caught in it. He says Indigenous Rights and Title to lands and resources need to be recognized and that an agreement should be negotiated that creates a future with more First Nations involvement—an agreement that works for the province, for the country and for Indigenous Peoples.

In the meantime, he also suggests a formula could be put in place with a template designed for use regardless of the size of the First Nations community to ensure funding and resources. The Tsilhqot'in Nation as a third level of government within its territory would be involved in decision making and revenue sharing, provincially and nationally.

"There's no quick solution. But if there's communication and co-operation, resolving the land question is doable. Reconciliation can happen if everyone's motivated to make it happen."

Chief **Judy Wilson** comes from a long line of First Nations Chiefs and leaders, including her father, Grand Chief Joe Manuel, and her late uncle, Grand Chief George Manuel, whose sons, Bob and Arthur, also served as Chiefs. As a teen-ager, Judy was often taken to rallies and meetings by her uncle George, where she soon learned about the frustrations of her people and the dependency that had been created by governments and First Nations' chronic underfunding.

By her mid-twenties Chief Judy was on council, and during the term she served with Uncle George, she learned even more. In 2007, she was elected Chief.

"When I was elected," she says, "our spiritual knowledge keepers explained to me that the Chief's role is like that of a grandmother or grandfather, who gathers information and brings it back to the people for discussion and to decide which direction they'll take. The Neskonlith band has long been well known for its political and on-the-land activism, as well as lobbying, and we continue with that.

"Also, some of the main work of our council has been to lessen government dependency and work towards self-reliance. Years ago, many of our people were not in favour of receiving government money when social welfare was brought in. They knew what it would do to them. It would make them obligated. We've dropped our social services dependency rate significantly through assistance programming to help those who need it to become more functional. We've increased education living allowances, so more people will choose the education way rather than the welfare way. But we need sustainable and long-term employment and business opportunities.

"I've travelled throughout Secwepemc territory, as well as provincially, nationally and internationally, listening and talking, but it's people like Andy and Phyllis Chelsea who kept us grounded as to who we are. They were invaluable within our Nation carrying and transmitting knowledge, language and information about our culture and sovereignty. I held Andy in high esteem for all that and still do."

Chief Judy says another area her First Nation is working on is economic development, which involves rights and title. "I became part of groups such as the Small Business Roundtable and [BC Rural Centre]. We lobbied and argued for a dividend fund to go back to rural regions and for recognition of rightful Secwepemc ownership of resources, lands and waters.

"Economic development is difficult because we do not have title to our reserves, even though Section 35 of the Canadian constitution recognizes and affirms Aboriginal rights—referred to as *inherent* title and rights by First Nations. We hold Certificates of Possession as a band and as band members, but not title. We are working strategically to change that and many other things. But the layers of bureaucracy at Indian Affairs with regard to change or development on a reserve mean it takes time, a lot of time. We're working on land designation to open up areas to more development or business, but being careful to avoid any negative impacts on our land or people. It's also important to us to have sustainable and 'green' economic strategies that are less fossil fuel dependent, avoid harming the earth but still bring opportunities to our members.

"Our Ancestral Chiefs laid out a comprehensive framework based on coexistence and a relationship with non-Natives on August 25, 1910, which was presented in written form to Sir Wilfrid Laurier during his visit to this area. It was called the *Memorial to Sir Wilfrid Laurier* and detailed things such as non-interference between settlers and First Nations with regard to laws and fair split of resources. Settlers were viewed as guests in our territory, but it was based on living together and sharing. That is our way of life—dividing what's available, taking care of people, leaving no one behind, enough for everyone."

She adds emphatically, "Community systems and functions need to be in place for First Nations Peoples. When I was first on council, there would be a crisis every day. We've worked with our people, encouraging personal independence, reducing debt and building a sense of community. Yes, there are still differences of opinion and opposition that exist within our community, but I think most people see the work that's been done, the progress that's been made. Some view band administration as an arm of the federal Indigenous Affairs Department. We're working to change that as it's mainly managing poverty—and although change can be unsettling, we cannot remain under the Indian Act."

Chief Judy and the council are hoping more young people will step forward and become involved with band and Nation issues, and are working towards that goal. She makes as much time as possible to attend Secwepemc Youth Council meetings. "I want to hear what they have to say and answer any questions they may have. Elders are providing guidance and direction too. Our youth are our tomorrow."

This Chief's opinion of Canada's justice system is understandably less than positive. "It's built on the Doctrine of Discovery, which declared Canada uninhabited, owned by no one, until its discovery by Europeans," she says. "Colonial principles and legislation still guide our courts, which are based on punitive thinking without restorative justice. However, there are Elders sitting with judges in some courts. Hopefully, improvements are being made not just for our people but for everyone who comes before the court.

"Jails do not rehabilitate. And there is a high percentage of Indigenous women incarcerated, besides men. I see young people going in and out of the system. When they return to our community, someone from our council likes to meet and talk with them. A lot of them are very hardened and angry with the system, the band, the council and their families. A lot more support is needed, both in and out of prison. For instance, was the sentence justifiable? Was there trauma in their lives? What rehab have they received? Gladue reports that explore a person's familial and past history definitely need to be put together for Indigenous accused—in fact, for all those charged with offences."

The seizure of Indigenous children is also a major issue for Chief Judy and her council. She reports that there are more Indigenous children in off-reserve care in Canada now than there were in residential schools. And she agrees with what her mother, Minnie Grinder, has always said: "It begins within the families."

"When intergenerational trauma is combined with alcohol and drugs and family breakdown, restoration takes time, effort and resources," Chief Judy says. "Support and preventative measures, such as parenting skills instruction, are absolutely necessary—as is funding. If parents grew up in an abusive institutionalized environment like a residential school, they have no positive role models to follow when it comes to their own children. And as a result of the suffering they endured, combined with the lack of employment, the family they create is weighed down by the yoke of poverty—yet another reason for their children to be seized."

Chief Judy recently attended an Interior Health meeting and brought up the issue of removal of Indigenous children from their homes. "I suggested there needs to be some sort of Gladue report system in these instances too, not just in criminal cases. There are incidents when social workers bring up things that happened to or with young mothers decades ago, something posted on Facebook, or they paint an unjustified but really bad picture of a mother when she's in court. I've seen it happen. And her children are removed.

"When parents and children are in trouble, we as a community step in. Grandparents and relatives are important to keeping the kids within their culture and family. We spend a lot of time rebuilding families. But that's where it has to start.

"The work Andy accomplished left us with a good legacy. His vision was a way forward. He and Phyllis based it on a treatment model. The first therapy centres were westernized. What the Chelseas and the Alkali Lake people did was indigenize them with our culture, our laws, our beliefs. When treatment is culturally appropriate following our ideologies, it works.

"As well, education is fundamental. My parents saw education as lifelong learning. We learn in universities and colleges, but when we come home, we must remember who we are, what our values and principles are. That combination will help to foster changes that are needed."

She continues, "I think the major issue for First Nations is self-determination. We have to get to that. And it could be different for every Nation. And another key factor is reconnecting to our land, the Secwepemc way of life, who we truly are. That can heal individuals and communities and promotes coming together.

"Part of self-determination involves implementation of the United Nations Declaration on the Rights of Indigenous Peoples, along with free and informed consent on issues. Perhaps the province fears that consent means a veto. But our people would work to define the Crown-Secwepemc relationship to come to mutually beneficial decisions. Discussion has to happen, both within bands and beyond. We need to understand each other and work towards the collective good. Bring it all to the circle and we'll get there."

Chief Judy recognizes that a lot of healing is needed, that long-standing grief needs to be confronted and soothed somehow. Old hurts and problems will need diligent work on both sides of the issues. The fractures caused by the Indian Act, racism and the imposition of reserve life require mending. Reconciliation provides a route, but it's really about a relationship that should have been established a very long time ago.

"I'm not giving up on self-determination," she says purposefully. "I know we'll achieve it one day. And nearby non-Native communities working with us will mean that the land will be better taken care of, and there'll be an improved community for all, inclusive, participatory and sustainable."

Appendix II

TREATIES AND LEGISLATION

HERE IS A LIST OF SOME TREATIES AND LEGISLATION BETWEEN Indigenous Peoples and Canada that I discovered while writing *Resolve*.

1600–1701
- Covenant Chain, early 1600s, the conventions and protocol origins of treaties
- Great Peace Treaty, signed at Montreal, 1701
- Treaty of Albany, 1701

1725–1752
- Peace and Friendship Treaties
- Boston Treaty
- Halifax Treaty

1754–1763 (Seven Years War, 1756–1763)
- Series of treaties with seven First Nations in Canada
- Britain's creation of the Indian Department in 1755
- Treaty of Oswegatchie, 1760

· Murray Treaty of Longueuil

Royal Proclamation of 1763

· This proclamation was issued by King George III of Great Britain as the basis of government in North American territories ceded by France to Britain in the Treaty of 1763 following the Seven Years War. It also set out the constitutional framework and protocols for treaty negotiations with Indigenous inhabitants.

· Its content states explicitly, in part: "And whereas it is just and reasonable and essential to our interest and the security of our colonies that the several nations or tribes of Indians with whom we are connected and who live under our protection should not be molested or disturbed in the possession of such parts of our Dominions and Territories as, not having been ceded to or purchased by us, are reserved to them or any of them, as their hunting grounds."

· While declaring western lands as exclusive hunting grounds for Indigenous Nations under his protection, the king claimed ultimate "dominion" over the entire region and prohibited any private person from buying Indigenous Lands, reserving that right of purchase for himself and his heirs, thus making the British Crown the sole agent in the transfer of Indigenous Lands to colonial settlers.

· In that it defined the North American interior west of the Appalachian Mountains as a vast Indigenous reserve, angering the Thirteen Colonies, the proclamation would contribute to the outbreak of the American Revolution in 1775.

- Section 35 of Canada's Constitution Act, 1982, affirms the Royal Proclamation as the basis for Crown-Indigenous treaties in Canada, and it continues to be applied to modern-day treaties.

1764–1867
- Colonial governments dispatch Indigenous peoples to reserves.
- The Treaty of Fort Stanwix, 1768, was the first based on the Royal Proclamation.
- The British government enacted the Quebec Act of 1774, favouring fur trade over land speculation, which would be a factor in the outbreak of the American Revolution.
- The conclusion of the American Revolution (1775–1783) preceded an arbitrary decision that redrew the map of North America and ignored Crown treaties with Indigenous peoples. In the Treaty of Paris, 1783, an international border was created dissecting the Great Lakes, completely disregarding the Covenant Chain and the Treaty of Fort Stanwix. First Nations were not part of the Paris negotiations even though their lands were at the heart of the dialogue.
- To address the resulting crisis, Quebec governor Frederick Haldimand made treaties with the Mississauga north of Lake Ontario in 1784 to set aside land along the Grand River and the Bay of Quinte for Six Nations peoples.
- Following the 1783 setback, treaty alliances eventually recovered, expanding and flourishing widely.

1790–1794
- Ohio Valley dispute and Jay Treaty

War of 1812

· The Treaty of Ghent, signed between Great Britain and America in Ghent, Belgium, in December 1814, agreed to end the war, that hostilities against First Nations would end, that captured territories would be returned and that prisoners would be released. However, western boundaries in North America remained unresolved until settled by a later commission.

1781–1862 Upper Canada Treaties

· Thirty treaties were negotiated in what would become Southwestern Ontario.
· Saugeen Peninsula Treaty
· Manitoulin Island Treaty
· Selkirk Treaty of 1817 (Manitoba)

1850

· Creation of twenty-four new reserves
· Robinson-Huron Treaty and Robinson-Superior Treaty with the Ojibwe—models for numbered treaties negotiated post-Confederation
· Initial payment of £4,000 and perpetual annuities of approximately £1,100, reserve land, plus hunting and fishing rights through the ceded territory

1850–1854

· Vancouver Island (Douglas) Treaties with fourteen First Nations
· As non-English speakers, Chiefs could not verify the terms on the paper they signed with an X, and they believed they

were agreeing to share, not cede, the 930 square kilometres of their territory, which they exchanged for clothing, cash and other goods.

1857 Gradual Civilization Act

· The Act to Encourage the Gradual Civilization of the Indian Tribes in the Province (of Canada), known as Upper and Lower Canada, was government policy designed to assimilate Indigenous Peoples and to foist the economic and social customs of European settler society upon them.
· It also encouraged enfranchisement of debt-free, educated Indigenous Peoples "of good moral character," which involved relinquishment of their Treaty Rights in exchange for land designated as homesteads and for voting privileges. It is reported that only one individual voluntarily chose this, an indication of the act's rejection by Indigenous Peoples.
· The Gradual Civilization Act led to further paternalistic laws such as the Gradual Enfranchisement Act of 1869.
· Both acts were consolidated under the Indian Act of 1876, which comprised existing imperial laws while disregarding Indigenous Rights as laid out in the Royal Proclamation of 1763.

1867 Post-Confederation

· With the creation of the Dominion of Canada in 1867, the British North America Act confirmed its federal government as responsible for "Indians and Lands reserved for Indians."
· In 1869, the Hudson's Bay Company, which had been created by royal charter in 1670 by Charles ɪɪ, sold its Rupert's

Land territory, covering one-third of what is Canada today, to the Canadian government for $1.5 million, thereby turning over control of all resources in the area, renamed the Northwest Territories. The transfer resulted in the assumption of governmental responsibility for the protection and well-being of the region's Indigenous Peoples, who saw it, however, as the sale of their lands without consent or consultation. For the Métis of the Red River Colony, this animosity would lead to open revolt.

· Various treaties were signed with Indigenous Nations in Northern Ontario, the Prairies, British Columbia and parts of the North, as part of Canadian expansion.

1871–1921

· Eleven Numbered Treaties were negotiated as the Canadian government sought to extend its sovereignty over western and northern Canada.
· Compensation to Indigenous Peoples for their Traditional Territories was also the purview of the Canadian government.
· Treaties seemingly evolved into agreements of economic practicality rather than recognition or involvement of Indigenous Rights.
· Indigenous Peoples sought recompense through treaties for the destruction of their way of life, notably the decimation of bison herds. However, provisions and goods promised were often delayed or never delivered.
· In 1876 the Indian Act was brought into force, consolidating previous colonial regulations aimed at destroying First Nations culture and promoting assimilation.

- The Indian Act was and is currently the principal statute through which the government manages and controls all aspects of the lives of Indigenous Peoples within Canada.

1923 Williams Treaties

- The Chippewa and Mississauga Peoples of the Simcoe and northern Lake Ontario regions continued their decades-long struggle to have the government recognize errors in early colonial treaties around allotment of lands and ceding of lands. A 1916 investigation and a 1923 federal and provincial Williams Commission confirmed such errors.
- Because the government had opened up the areas in question to non-Indigenous settlement and exploitation of natural resources, the Chippewa Treaty was negotiated in 1923 covering lands from Georgian Bay to the Ottawa River. The second treaty with the Mississauga also signed that year involved lands from Lake Simcoe to the shore of Lake Ontario. In these treaties, which included financial payment for boundary adjustments, the First Nations surrendered not only title to the land but also their hunting and fishing rights—a substantial change from earlier treaties.

1920s–1970s Land Title and Rights

- In Ontario and the Prairies, Indigenous Treaties were the foundation of land tenure. Elsewhere, non-Indigenous settlement, for the most part, proceeded without the negotiation for Indigenous Title.
- Indigenous Peoples were allocated reserves and were under direct control of the federal government even without treaties.

1969 White Paper and the Nisga'a Treaty

· In that the Nisga'a people of British Columbia's Nass River valley had never surrendered title to their homelands, beginning in 1969 they brought to the courts their opposition to the province's stand that Indigenous Peoples did not hold inherent rights.

· The federal government's 1969 White Paper on Indigenous policy that proposed ending treaties and the removal of special status for Indigenous Peoples resulted in widespread resistance as well as cohesive activism by First Nations and the eventual abandonment of the White Paper by government.

· In 1976, the Nisga'a and the government began treaty negotiations. Fourteen years later, in 1990, they reached a preliminary agreement and the province joined the discussions. The agreement was finalized in 1996.

· In 2000, the Nisga'a attained control of two thousand square kilometres of their ancestral territory and self-government under which the Indian Act ceased to apply and the Nation had legal authority to conduct its affairs and pass its own laws.

1975 to Present

· 1975 James Bay and Northern Quebec Agreement with Cree and Inuit
· 1978 Northeastern Quebec Agreement with the Schefferville Naskapi
· The Sechelt Indian Band Self-Government Act was enacted in 1986.

- In 1990, Elijah Harper, an Oji-Cree MLA from Manitoba, blocked comprehensive revisions to the Canadian Constitution proposed without Indigenous representation at Meech Lake.
- Also in 1990, the Mohawk of Kanesatake challenged the town council of Oka over a proposed golf course and condo expansion on what had been a Mohawk burial ground, resulting in an armed seventy-eight-day standoff, a military fatality and the wounding of a First Nations girl. The development was halted; the federal government purchased the land in question, but the issue of who holds title to the land has never been resolved.
- The Inherent Right to Self-Government Policy of 1995 was established to negotiate practical arrangements with First Nations to bring self-government to fruition, while recognizing that no single form of government would be applicable to all Indigenous communities. Seventeen self-government agreements were agreed upon over the next fifteen years.
- The Indian Residential Schools Settlement Agreement, between legal counsel for former students, churches, the Assembly of First Nations, Indigenous organizations and the Government of Canada, was approved in 2006 and its implementation commenced in September 2007.
- Canada's Truth and Reconciliation Commission was established in 2008 and in 2015 submitted its final report, which included ninety-four calls to action.
- The National Inquiry into Missing and Murdered Indigenous Women and Girls commenced its work in September 2016.

- Indigenous and Northern Affairs Canada was split into two departments—Crown-Indigenous Relations and Northern Affairs Canada, and Indigenous Services Canada—in August 2017.
- Government initiatives from 2015 to 2017 included an agreement to support Indigenous Survivors of the Sixties Scoop, implementation of additional Truth and Reconciliation Commission recommendations, elimination of all First Nations drinking water restrictions (boil water advisories) with twenty-seven lifted as of December 2017, increased funding to Indigenous communities and inclusion in Canada's citizenship oath of the pledge to honour Indigenous treaties.
- In addition to the above, thirty-six agreements and letters of understanding were negotiated with Indigenous organizations and Nations between April 2016 and November 2017.
- The federal government budget in February 2018 increased funding to $1.1 billion annually for First Nations self-government and governance structures outside the authoritarian and restrictive Indian Act, as well as for services, such as child welfare, health care, housing and water, bringing total federal expenditure on Indigenous files to $2.56 billion per year.

1977–1982

Canadian Constitution Repatriation and the Charter of Rights and Freedoms

- First Nations, Inuit and Métis political organizations were excluded from negotiations concerning repatriation of the Canadian constitution.

- Indigenous and Treaty Rights were omitted from a 1981 proposal concerning the Canadian Charter of Rights and Freedoms.
- Lobbying and pressure by Indigenous groups resulted in two clauses being added to the charter that recognized "existing aboriginal and treaty rights" and included a definition of First Nations, Inuit and Métis.
- The undefined "existing aboriginal and treaty rights" were the topic of conferences between 1983 and 1987 in an attempt to delineate those rights. No consensus was reached.
- The lack of clarity around critical aspects of Indigenous Rights within the Charter of Rights and Freedoms has compelled Indigenous groups to turn to the courts for resolution, where several judgments have defined rights, title and treaty parameters. More adjudication around this issue will undoubtedly be required in the future.

Modern-Day Treaties in Northern Canada
- Nunavut Land Claims Agreement, 1993
- Sahtu Dene and Métis Comprehensive Land Claim Agreement, 1993
- Eleven Yukon First Nations negotiated treaties, 1993–2005
- Tlicho Land Claims and Self-Government Agreement, 2003, central Northwest Territories
- The foregoing agreements and treaties facilitated Indigenous municipal and corporate structures, and also First Nations participation as shareholders in natural resources extraction.

Modern-Day Treaties in British Columbia

· In 1991, treaty negotiations began between federal and provincial governments and some First Nations in British Columbia.
· Tsawwassen First Nation agreement finalized, 2009
· Maa-nulth First Nations agreement, 2011
· Tla'amin agreement, 2016
· In 2014, the Tsilhqot'in First Nation won its Supreme Court of Canada case, started in 1989, which restored title rights to 1,700 square kilometres of their traditional land and included benefits, profits and the requirement of their prior consent to any economic development in their area.

Modern-Day Treaties in Quebec and Labrador

· Labrador Inuit Land Claims Agreement (Nunatsiavut region), 2005
· Nunavik Inuit Land Claims Agreement (northern Quebec), 2006
· Eeyou Marine Region Land Claims Agreement (Hudson Bay), 2010
· Innu of Labrador treaty, 2011, regarding Voisey's Bay vast nickel deposit

Treaties and the United Nations (UN)

· In 1987, the United Nations Working Group on Indigenous Populations commenced a global study of "treaties, agreements and other constructive arrangements between states and Indigenous populations."

- The UN General Assembly, in September 2007, adopted its *Declaration on the Rights of Indigenous Peoples.*
- Article 37 of the declaration reads: "Indigenous peoples have the right to the recognition, observance and enforcement of treaties, agreements and other constructive arrangements concluded with States or their successors and to have States honour and respect such treaties, agreements and other constructive arrangements."
- In 2016, Canada fully endorsed the UN declaration.
- In January 2019, a UN Human Rights Committee decision stated that Canada is obligated to remove from the Indian Act discrimination against First Nations women and their descendants to ensure they are granted Indian status on the same basis as First Nations men and their descendants.[1]

---

1   Deer, "Indian Act Still Discriminates against First Nations Women."

BIBLIOGRAPHY

INTERVIEWS

In conversation or correspondence with the author.

Antoine, Frank. November 2017.

Birchwater, Sage. October 2017.

Chelsea, Andy. January to June 2017.

Chelsea, Ivy. May 2018.

Chelsea, Kevin. By email. May 2018.

Chelsea, Owen. By email. May 2018.

Chelsea, Phyllis. May 2017 to March 2019.

Chelsea, Robert. May 2018.

Dufour, Lorne. By letter. October 2017.

French, Diana. July 2017.

Gladue, Dean. December 2017.

Johnson, Dorothy. December 2018.

Johnson, Irvine. December 2017.

Johnson, Julianna. December 2018.

Jules, Ronnie. December 2017.

Mountain, Tammy. November 2017.

Ross, David. December 2018.

Wilson, Judy. February 2018.

BOOKS

Birchwater, Sage. Foreword to *Jacob's Prayer*, by Lorne
    Dufour. Halfmoon Bay, BC: Caitlin Press, 2009.

Dupuis, Jenny Kay, and Kathy Kacer. *I Am Not a Number*.
    Toronto: Second Story Press, 2016.

Haig-Brown, Celia. *Resistance and Renewal: Surviving
    the Indian Residential School*. 6th printing. Vancouver:
    Arsenal Pulp Press Ltd., 1993.

Johnston, Patrick. *Native Children and the Child Welfare
    System*. Toronto: Lorimer, 1983.

MacAndrew, Craig, and Robert B. Edgerton. *Drunken
    Comportment: A Social Explanation*. Hawthorne, NY:
    Aldine, 1969.

Martens, Tony, Brenda Daily and Maggie Hodgson. *The
    Spirit Weeps: Characteristics and Dynamics of Incest and
    Child Sexual Abuse with a Native Perspective*. Edmonton:
    Ncchi Institute, 1988.

Robertson, David Alexander. *Sugar Falls: A Residential
    School Story*. Illus. Scott B. Henderson. Winnipeg:
    Highwater Press, 2011.

Sellars, Bev. *They Called Me Number One: Secrets and
    Survival at an Indian Residential School*. 9th printing.
    Vancouver: Talonbooks, 2016.

ARTICLES, MAGAZINES, NEWSPAPERS

Brown, Ian. "Confronting Race, Shame and Reconciliation at Sea in the Far North." *Globe and Mail.* Article published October 28, 2017; updated November 12, 2017.

Canadian Press. "Mounties Raped, Abused BC Aboriginal Girls, Rights Watchdog Alleges in Report." *National Post,* February 13, 2013.

Dyck, Roland, Nathaniel Osgood, Ting Hsiang Lin, Amy Gao and Mary Rose Stang. "Epidemiology of Diabetes Mellitus among First Nations and Non-First Nations Adults." *Canadian Medical Association Journal* 182, no. 3 (February 2010): 249–56.

Edwards, Kyle. "Fighting Foster Care." *Maclean's,* January 2016.

———. "Canadian Injustice." *Maclean's,* November 2017.

Frank, John W., Roland S. Moore and Genevieve M. Ames. "Historical and Cultural Roots of Drinking Problems among American Indians." *American Journal of Public Health* 90, no. 3 (March 2000).

Grant, Tavia. "Report Submitted to Ottawa Highlights Police Abuse Against Indigenous Women." *Globe and Mail,* June 19, 2017.

Lavallee, Trudy. "Honouring Jordan: Putting First Nations Children First and Funding Fights Second." *Paediatrics & Child Health* 10, no. 9 (November 2005): 527–29.

Mason, Gary. "The Punishing Sixties Scoop." *Globe and Mail,* February 16, 2017.

Mccardle, Bennett. "Enfranchisement." In *Canadian Encyclopedia.* Article published February 7, 2006; last edited September 25, 2014.

Miller, J.R., and Tabitha Marshall. "Residential Schools in
    Canada." In *Canadian Encyclopedia*. Article published
    October 10, 2012; last edited June 14, 2018.
"The Oldest Cattle Ranch in B.C." *Canadian Cowboy
    Country*, 2010.
Sinclair, Niigaanwewidam James, and Sharon Dainard.
    "Sixties Scoop." In *Canadian Encyclopedia*. Article
    published June 22, 2016; last edited February 15, 2017.

REPORTS

Aguiar, William, and Regine Halseth. *Aboriginal Peoples
    and Historic Trauma: The Processes of Intergenerational
    Transmission*. Prince George, BC: National Collaborating
    Centre for Aboriginal Health, 2015.
*Submission to the Government of Canada on Police Abuse
    of Indigenous Women in Saskatchewan and Failures to
    Protect Indigenous Women from Violence*. Human Rights
    Watch, June 19, 2017.
Truth and Reconciliation Commission of Canada. *Honouring
    the Truth, Reconciling for the Future: Summary of the
    Final Report of the Truth and Reconciliation Commission
    of Canada*. Winnipeg: Truth and Reconciliation
    Commission of Canada, 2015.
UN General Assembly. Resolution 61/295. United Nations
    Declaration on the Rights of Indigenous Peoples. A/
    RES/67/295. October 2, 2007.

WEBSITES, RADIO BROADCASTS AND BLOGS

"Aboriginal People and Alcohol: Not a Genetic Predisposition." CBC News, May 30, 2014.

An Act to Amend the Indian Act in Response to the Superior Court of Quebec Decision in Descheneaux c. Canada. Bill S-3. Parliament of Canada website, December 12, 2017.

Barnsley, Paul. "Church Considering Request to Rescind Doctrine of Discovery." APTN National News, June 1, 2016.

Barrera, Jorge. "Budget Boosts Funding for First Nations Self-Government, Indigenous Services." CBC News, February 27, 2018.

"Complaints and Allegations Against Police." In *Human Rights and Policing: Creating and Sustaining Organizational Change*. Ontario Human Rights Commission website.

Crey, Karrmen. "Enfranchisement." Indigenous Foundations website, First Nations and Indigenous Studies, University of British Columbia. https://indigenousfoundations.arts.ubc.ca/enfranchisement/.

Deer, Jessica. "Indian Act Still Discriminates against First Nations Women, Says UN Human Rights Committee." CBC News, January 17, 2019.

"Esk'etemc Declaration of Title and Rights." Esk'et First Nation website, May 8, 2017. http://www.esketemc.ca/esketemc-declaration-of-title-rights/.

"Indigenous Nurses Call Out Systemic Racism with Life-or-Death Consequences." In *The Current*. CBC Radio, March 2, 2018.

Leamon, Sarah E. "Canada Has Its Own Demons When It Comes to Police Brutality." *Huffington Post*, October 13, 2016.

McDiarmid, Margo. "Indigenous Communities Embracing Clean Energy, Creating Thousands of Jobs." CBC News, October 11, 2017.

"Our History, Our Health," First Nations Health Authority. http://www.fnha.ca/wellness/our-history-our-health.

Palmater, Pamela. "Police Violence in Ontario Has Reached a Crisis Level and We Should Be Very Upset." *Rabble.ca*, February 2, 2016.

"RCMP Accused of Rape in Report on BC Aboriginal Women." CBC News, February 13, 2013.

"RCMP Statement on Human Rights Watch Report." Royal Canadian Mounted Police, June 19, 2017.

"RCMP Response to Chairperson-Initiated Complaint and Public Interest Investigation into Policing in Northern British Columbia." Royal Canadian Mounted Police, February 16, 2017.

Reith, Terry. "'Be Proud of Who You Are': Indigenous Elders Offer Advice to the Young about Self-Respect and Reconciliation." CBC News, September 30, 2017.

Spear, Wayne K. "Indian Residential Schools." *Wayne K. Spear* (blog), March 10, 2010.

———. "Everything You Need to Know about Canada's Indian Residential Schools." *Wayne K. Spear* (blog), February 25, 2013.

Szalavitz, Maia. "No, Native Americans Aren't Genetically More Susceptible to Alcoholism." *The Verge*, October 2, 2015.

ABOUT THE AUTHOR

Photo James Mintz

Carolyn Parks Mintz is an author, freelance journalist and public speaker and was twice nominated as a Woman of Distinction. She was the content specialist of the 1997 video *I Will Walk This Road With You*, the producer, writer and host of the radio talk show *Ontario's West Coast Today* in 2008 and authored *The Eye of the Dragon: Women, Cancer and Courage* (EbbTide Publishing, 2004), for which she received the Global Calgary Woman of Vision award.